LATIMER BRIEFING 09

WITNESSING TO WESTERN MUSLIMS

A WORLDVIEW APPROACH TO WESTERN FAITH

BY RICHARD SHUMACK

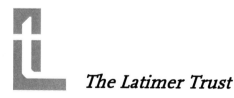

The Latimer Trust

Published by the Latimer Trust June 2011

The Latimer Trust (formerly Latimer House, Oxford) is a conservative Evangelical research organisation within the Church of England, whose main aim is to promote the history and theology of Anglicanism as understood by those in the Reformed tradition. Interested readers are welcome to consult its website for further details of its many activities.

The Latimer Trust
PO Box 26685, London N14 4XQ UK
Registered Charity: 1084337
Company Number: 4104465
Web: www.latimertrust.org
E-mail: administrator@latimertrust.org

THIS BOOK IS FOR YOU IF YOU ARE A CHRISTIAN WHO

...has Muslim friends, neighbours or workmates.
...wants to understand how Muslims think about God.
...finds formulaic approaches to witnessing inadequate.
...feels under equipped to share your faith with Muslims.

"This small book is a goldmine of wisdom and experience gathered from Richard's many years of ministry. It invites us to break through simple stereotypes and invites us to think hard about what it is to understand and reach out to people who may be different from us in faith and culture. At the same time it encourages us to see that reaching out like this is not beyond any of us."

Greg Anderson, Head of Mission Department,
Moore Theological College, Sydney.

Richard has provided a valuable service to those involved in outreach to Muslims. This book is a unique and insightful contribution to the field. I thoroughly recommend it.

Bernie Power, Lecturer, Centre for the Study of Islam
and Other Faiths, Melbourne School of Theology.

CONTENTS

Dedicated with thanks to all who have partnered with me in witnessing Christ.

Introduction

"Be warned my Son...of making many books there is no end..."

Ecclesiastes 12:12

This is a book about Christians witnessing Christ to Muslims. It is written for any Christian seeking to be better equipped to share their faith with a Muslim friend, neighbour, workmate, sporting team mate, or for any church seeking to minister to local Muslim communities. But there are already plenty of books about ministry among Muslims. There are books about understanding Islam, books comparing Christianity and Islam, books sharing testimonies of Muslims coming to faith in Christ, and books about how to share your faith with Muslims. So, why write another one?

Like many things this book grows out of a need. I have spent the last decade living and ministering in a mainly Muslim local community in a large Western city. Over the years I have kept an eye out for resources to help our ministry, but I have discovered resource gaps. Many of the ministry experiences I have had, and many of the questions I have asked, are not being talked about by the books I read. I believe these gaps are to do with people sharing the experience of living with, and witnessing to, Western Muslims. By Western Muslims I mean Muslims who have either been brought up in, or have spent a significant part of their life living in, Western countries.[1]

It seems to me that most of the books written about Christian ministry to Muslims fall into two areas. On the one hand, there are many books written by missionaries who write from their mission

---

[1] I am thinking here particularly of the U.S.A., the U.K., Western Europe, Canada, New Zealand and Australia.

experience. These are usually people who have lived in a Muslim country and who understand Muslims, in one particular Muslim context, very deeply. Unfortunately for me, the world they describe is very different from the world I live and minister in. My Muslim neighbours do not live in a Muslim country and the cultural worlds they experience are mixed and complicated – they are Western Muslims. The freedoms and taboos of their faith communities are very different to those in the Muslim world. Their understanding of Jesus, and Christianity, is very different to that of Muslims who are encountered in the traditional missionary experience. Many of the approaches to witnessing Christ that I read about in these books do not seem to be very effective in my Western context. The other thing about books written by missionaries is that they tend to be helpful if you have a similar ministry as a missionary, meaning someone who moves around witnessing as a job. My question, though, is: how do you witness when you are simply a long term neighbour, or workmate, of a Western Muslim?

On the other hand there are some books written for a Western context. But I find that often these are about Islam as a religion, rather than Muslims. These books tend to be written for a Christian audience largely ignorant of Islam, and often written as a warning of the dangers of Islamic agendas. These books are usually very helpful for understanding what orthodox Muslims are supposed to believe, and how they are supposed to live. They can provide great insight into the theological and political issues at stake in the Christian encounter with Islam. Again, however, these books leave me with questions. My experience is that Western Muslims are extremely varied both in what they believe and in how they live out their Islamic faith. It is one thing to understand traditional Islamic theology, a whole different thing to see how Muslims try (or don't try!) to make Islam work in a modern Western city. Also, these books are great if you want to debate theology with a Muslim. But, again, if the Muslim is your neighbour, what happens when the theological debate reaches a stalemate? Does witness end there?

The gap I see, then, is in coming to terms with witnessing to Western Muslim neighbours. What I hope to do in this book is to attempt to fill some of that gap by providing a witnessing framework for any Christian living in the West who lives next to, works, studies or plays with Muslims. The ideas here come very much out of my personal reflection, and of course not everyone in Muslim ministry will agree with all of my thoughts or emphases. Similarly the ideas grew out of my particular ministry and community context and will no doubt be partly limited to that. I believe, however, that this book, at least broadly, asks the right questions and gives solid principles for anyone to look in good directions for answers to those questions.

To give a brief roadmap: I hope that after reading chapter one you will have a deeper understanding of how Western Muslims view the world. I hope after reading chapter two you will understand some of the key beliefs that many Western Muslims tend to have which create barriers to witness that need negotiating. I hope that after reading chapter three you will be encouraged to be an intentional neighbour; living a life of grace in ways that helpfully point your Muslim neighbour to the source of that grace. And I hope that after reading chapter four you will be confident of finding ways of speaking about your faith that move beyond the usual superficial theological debates, into a deep sharing of faith.

1. Thinking...

*"If you make people think they're thinking, they'll love you;
But if you really make them think, they'll hate you."*

Don Marquis

It is hard work to think hard (obviously)! It would be easy in a book like this to cut to the chase and give ten easy, practical steps to witnessing to Muslims. Many seminars on Muslim ministry I have attended reduce witness to this, as well as many of the missionary books I mentioned. There is nothing wrong with practical ministry tips – we will get to the practical stuff in chapters three and four – but I want to encourage you not to jump straight there, but to start with some hard work thinking about what is required when witnessing Christ to Muslims.

Here is an example of why. In my early days of witnessing to Muslims I went to visit a newly arrived Muslim refugee. I had never met him, but had been asked to visit him to welcome him to our country and to see how we might be able to help him and his family settle in. When I arrived at his home at the arranged time, he welcomed me in, and then led me past the empty living room, and into a spare bedroom where he asked me to sit on the bed. He then left the room, and returned a few minutes later with a small chair. He then asked me to move and sit on the chair, and then with no explanation left the room again. He was gone for maybe fifteen minutes, and I was left wondering what was happening. I wondered why I was left in the bedroom. I wondered whether maybe there were others in the house using the other rooms, but there weren't. I wondered whether he was away praying or making tea, but he wasn't.

So I waited on the chair. Eventually he returned and we began to talk. Soon we got on to religion and he asked me to explain my faith to him. He had heard of the Bible but had never read one so I arranged to come back and bring him a Bible. A few days later I

4

returned with a Bible and once again we ended up talking in the bedroom. Again he asked me to explain who I thought Jesus was so I opened up Mark chapter 1 (because it was the simplest gospel) and we started reading together from the first verse: "The beginning of the gospel about Jesus Christ, the Son of God..." That was as far as we got. He refused to read any further because he could not accept that Jesus was the Son of God. Shortly after he had asked me to leave and I was standing outside his house, still wondering. Where had I gone wrong? Had I said the wrong thing? Had I behaved inappropriately? Was Mark 1 a bad passage to read? Was he simply not open to hearing about Jesus? And why were we always meeting in the bedroom? I was left with many questions about his beliefs, his culture and our attempts to communicate.

Muslims are simply people, but people are not simple. People are complicated in their beliefs, their cultures and their ways of communicating. Similarly the gospel is simple enough for a child, but profound enough to touch people's hearts in myriads of ways. When it is communicated effectively the gospel, too, both resonates with and challenges beliefs and cultures. It is these complex issues of belief, culture and communication that we need to think hard about when we seek to reach Muslims for Christ. You will have to think hard in this chapter, but I promise it will be worth it!

1.1.   Thinking about "understanding" others

Christians are called to love their neighbours. More than that, we are called to reach out to our neighbours who live all the way out to the ends of the earth (Matthew 28:16-20, Mark 13:10, Acts 1:8). That includes our Muslim neighbours, especially when the 'ends of the earth' turns out to be our street or workplace. As part of loving we are called to persuade our neighbours that life with Jesus is the best way to go. This has an uncomfortable edge to it because it involves persuading our neighbours that all our lives – theirs included – have serious deficiencies and require transformation through faith in Christ (Romans 3:21-26). In short, we seek to persuade people with different beliefs to us (about Jesus at least) to change those beliefs.

There are many things that can make this encounter difficult, but an important one is our natural tendency, deep down, to think that we are normal. Of course we have no way of describing what normal is, but we still tend to think that whatever "normal" is, we are it. We tend to think that the way we think is the obvious way to think. We tend to think that the way we approach doing life, is the sensible way to do life – even when we struggle to pull it off!

This wouldn't matter except that there are people who think and act differently from us. They like different things. They believe different things. And yet we tend to feel that people who are like us are the other normal people, and we don't naturally or quickly understand why others think or act differently. In addition, most of us tend to be lazy and not to put a lot of effort into understanding where other people are coming from. This is understandable as sometimes it is difficult enough to comprehend people who are a lot like us – even in my marriage there are times we don't need to speak because we know what each other is thinking; but there are other times when I wonder if I am living with an alien. It is even tougher with people who are very different from us. I might put some effort into understanding the menu in my local Indian restaurant because I can easily grasp how good Indian food tastes, but understanding the impact of the Caste system in Indian society is a whole different ball game.

For most people, most of the time, a lack of understanding of different people has not necessarily been a huge problem. Historically people have lived in largely mono-cultural situations where most people, a few "weirdos" aside, were considered to be fairly normal. But the world has changed. Western countries are now "multi": multi-cultural, multi-racial, multi-linguistic, multi-religious. Even so, most of us in our multi-cultural world just live and let live. We might enjoy the different cuisines, movies or music now available to us (or at least Westernised versions of them), or play the tourist at a fun cultural celebration, but that's about it.

Christians seeking to share Christ with people to the ends of the earth, however, are called to a much deeper encounter with people. It is one thing to ask people why their naan bread tastes better when it is cooked in a Tandoor oven, but a whole different thing to question the whole basis for their life.

As I observe Christian encounters with Islam it seems to me that many miss the mark due to a lack of understanding of where people are coming from, on both sides of the encounter. One example of this is the writing of the well known Muslim apologist Ahmed Deedat. One of his most popular books is called "Is the Bible God's Word?", and in it he criticises the Bible for a variety of reasons including apparent historical inconsistencies and theological problems. It is clear that Deedat knew the Bible exceptionally well (it is claimed he had memorized it!). The problem with the book is that while he knew lots about the Bible, in the end he did not "get" the Bible. This was because instead of understanding and evaluating the Bible on its own terms, he was always viewing it through a Muslim framework, and measuring it by Muslim standards.

In the end his critique of the Bible came down to this: the Bible is not the Word of God because it is not like the Qur'an. This critique is like me saying "Your dog is not a pet, because it is not like my axolotl". This sort of argument misses the mark because the problem is not with your dog, but with my wrong understanding of what a pet is. Similarly Deedat's argument fails because the problem is not with the Bible, but with his misunderstanding of how Christians view the Bible as God's Word.

My fear is that many Christians do the same thing as Deedat in reverse when encountering Islam. We fail to try and stand in the shoes of Muslims and understand where they are coming from when they think about God and faith. Then we criticise them for not thinking about God like us, or not getting it quickly and easily when we explain our faith on our terms, out of our own assumptions about God, and using our theological language. To understand where someone is coming from enough to speak truth deeply into their world view takes hard work, and, in the case of Islam, hard work in understanding why it is they believe what they do.

1.2.   Thinking about belief

Everyone has a belief system, but very few people take the opportunity to reflect deeply on how they came to those beliefs. Our beliefs arise out of many sources. Some arise out of direct sense experience of the world; for example, my belief that my car is red. Some we might come to intuitively; such as, the belief that I need love. Some (although many fewer than we would like to think) grow out of systematic thinking; like my understanding of how the brakes on my bike work. Some might grow out of trial and error in making life work. Some, in fact the vast majority of beliefs, come from what other people tell us is true. Belief then is not simple.

In fact, it gets more complicated again. First, the different sources of belief are not independent of each other. For example, we will usually believe the testimony of someone we trust, but at the same time we will be looking for that testimony to fit with our experience, or our gut feelings. Second, all of us will have different ways of putting the sources together, or attach different weights (or authority) to certain sources. Some of us are predominantly gut thinkers; for example, I have many optimistic gut beliefs about my golf game that lead me constantly to try shots that logic tells me have never, and probably will never, work. In my golf beliefs, intuition overrides logic. Some of us are practical thinkers, and we build our beliefs mainly out of what works, even if those beliefs are contradictory. So I might believe that lying is always wrong, except when it gets me out of trouble. Some of us are followers, who tend to believe what our teachers tell us, even if it goes against what seems to make sense to us. Some of us might be sceptics who tend to doubt anything we cannot prove for ourselves. All of us will be slightly different in how our belief systems are made up.

All this is true of our beliefs about God too. Our beliefs about God might arise out of direct experience (for example, a miracle, or a mystical experience); a gut feeling that there must be a creator; systematic thinking about the historical evidence for Jesus; or the testimony of witnesses to God's action (whether they are prophets or friends who have experienced God in some way). Again our beliefs

8

about God will usually arise out of a mixture of all these (and other) sources, and again we will all attach different weights to the relative importance of each of them.

By now you may be thinking it is getting a little too complicated! But the point of all this is to help us to realise that whenever we sit down and talk to someone about their beliefs, there are many things going on for them. Conversation tends to focus on our systematic thinking, but the beliefs talked about will have come from many different sources, and challenging those beliefs will involve criticizing those sources, some of which are held very dear. For example, if my main source of knowledge about God was from my beloved dead uncle, who was the most wonderful man I ever knew and is above criticism, then be careful before challenging me! If you are serious in wanting to engage people in a discussion about their deepest held beliefs then you will need to go deep with them to understand what authorities undergird their beliefs. There is no point simply suggesting that you are right about something because you have a logical argument for it, when your hearer puts far more stock in their gut feeling about the issue. On the other hand your testimony about how much joy you feel when you pray will carry little weight with someone who believes faith is a serious matter, supported primarily by authoritative traditions.

To illustrate this in the Christian encounter with Islam, take the example of the Muslim belief that the Bible has been changed. This is an interesting belief for two reasons. First, it is held by nearly every Muslim I have met on the basis of someone else's testimony – usually the community tradition. I am yet to meet a Muslim who has actually looked first hand into the primary sources concerning the textual history of the Bible (or the Qur'an for that matter!). For most Muslims this is not a systematic, thought-out belief, and yet when addressing this belief most Christians give systematic thought-out answers that Muslims either don't understand, or are not interested in.

Second, even when you find a Muslim who is interested in having a systematic discussion about the textual history of the Bible, you will find that they usually have a very different understanding of

9

how to establish historical reliability. For most Muslims, historical reliability is found in the establishment of an unbroken chain of transmission in which all the testifiers are known and trusted. Unbroken transmission provides the key basis for belief that a text is unchanged (they claim to have such reliability with the Qur'an). In contrast, Christians generally point to the vast array of independent texts of varying age available that point to the reliability of the Bible text as we have it today. Muslims tend not to be interested in this: for them one text is enough if it has been passed down well, and the Bible fails this test because Christians can neither say with certainty who wrote large parts of it (for example, the book of Hebrews), nor point to unbroken lines of transmission. As a result, Christian and Muslim beliefs concerning the reliability of the Bible come both from different sources, and from different frameworks for establishing such beliefs. This makes for a tricky conversation!

Another important example of how this works out in the Christian/Muslim context is the level of value placed on the degree to which beliefs should be *sensible*. In traditional Islam, a human is essentially a rational, thinking being who knows God through his or her mind accepting God's laws and obeying them. Muslims value incredibly highly the idea that Islam is sensible because its theology of God is clear and simple (God is one), its scriptures are complete and completely divine, and the rules for life are laid out comprehensively and just need following. In contrast, most Muslims look at Christianity and see nonsense. They see that most of the central beliefs of Christianity are unexplainable: how God can be three and one, how Jesus can be God and man, how the Bible can be both divine and human in its authorship, and how justification and sanctification can be now and not yet, all by grace and yet with our effort. Of course there are many other reasons why Muslims and Christians hold their particular beliefs on God, Jesus and scripture, but whether beliefs match up to common sense is most highly valued by Muslims. Again this makes for tricky conversation.

Perhaps by now you are thinking this is all too hard, but don't panic! Understanding people enough to speak meaningfully to them about beliefs is tricky and takes hard work, but it is not

insurmountable. I will consider how to talk about ⸯ
issues in chapter four. But there is one last complicatic
think about first.

1.3. *Thinking about culture*

Just when you thought things were already too complicated, let me
add in a third factor to consider: culture. There are all sorts of ways of
defining and experiencing culture – I have already mentioned food,
music, etc. – but we need to understand that culture is very closely
tied to beliefs. I have talked about the different ways people come to
their beliefs, but the same process is true of cultures as a whole as
well. This is not a great surprise when cultures are largely made up of
groups of similar people. Like different people, different cultures
attach different weights to different sources of beliefs. Traditional
cultures tend to give a lot of weight to the testimony of elders or
authorities, and very little weight to individual systematic thinking. By
contrast, recent Western culture has tended to give a lot of weight to
systematic or scientific thought, and less to intuition, or tradition.

This link between culture and belief is especially important to
grasp in the case of Islam. Islam is not just a set of private religious
beliefs. Islam is a way of life that seeks to transform all of society into
that way of life, reflecting the life of the early Muslim community
under Muhammad's leadership. Traditional Islam then, seeks to
create a society that largely reflects the cultural values – including the
belief frameworks – of seventh century Arab tribal culture. Such
culture places high value on many of the belief sources we have
already mentioned such as the testimony of authoritative elders over
independent reasoning, and the reliability of aural transmission over
historical artefacts.

The current situation in the West is that most Muslims you
meet will have some sort of cultural background from a Muslim
society – even if they were born in the West. As Islam has influenced
different cultures over time, however, it has been increasingly hard to
distinguish between what is Islamic, and what is cultural. This means
that if you really want to understand where Muslims are coming from

it is usually not enough to understand Islam or the Muslim mindset. You also need to work hard at appreciating their particular culture.

One cultural issue you will usually encounter is *shame and honour*. A powerful example of this was seen in the 2006 World Cup final between France and Italy. Frenchman Zinedine Zidane was the best player in the world at the time. He was elegant, skilful and the key to France's hopes of winning the cup. He was also from a North African Muslim background. Towards the end of the match, an Italian opponent made an abusive comment to Zidane about his family. Zidane felt this profoundly dishonoured his family, and responded by head-butting his opponent. The result of this action was that Zidane was sent off, and France lost the final. This match was the culmination of Zidane's entire personal football career and, more than that, he represented the hopes of an entire nation. Yet after the loss, he had no regrets about his actions because he had defended his family's honour. Zidane's *shame and honour* culture had profoundly influenced his beliefs: both about what was of greatest value in life (family honour), and what was required to protect those values (vanquishing an opponent).

In using this example I am not saying that every Muslim would act this way or even that it is necessarily a Muslim way of acting. What I am saying is that *shame and honour* was valued extremely highly in Muhammad's culture, and that it is therefore generally valued extremely highly in most Muslim cultures. This is one example of a cultural issue but there are many others. Such issues require us to spend time appreciating how our Muslim neighbours' cultures work.

1.4.   Thinking about persuasion

So far we have thought about difference, belief and culture. All these are important because as Christians witnessing for Christ, we are seeking to speak, in word and deed, to hearts; and people's hearts are tied to their individual and cultural beliefs. Assuming, however, that we have done a good job of understanding where people are coming from – where Muslim hearts are at – how then do we speak persuasively to the heart? In order to think about this too, consider the following illustration.

Imagine you are a passionate basketball fan, and I am a passionate footy[2] fan (not hard for me to imagine!). If you want to persuade me that basketball is a much better game than football, how should you go about it? You could point out all the things you thought were bad about football: it can be violent and leave players with serious injuries; it is inherently sexist as it is predominantly male; there are many dubious characters playing the game with track records of abuse that have been plastered over the media; and so on. This may work if I have nagging dissatisfaction with football, but if I deeply love football it is more likely to lead to me pointing out the things I think are bad about basketball: the players are soft; it is a 'height-ist' game that discriminates against short people; and that there are plenty of misbehaving basketball players too. Instead you could try a different approach and point out all the things you liked about basketball: it is non-contact; it is fast scoring; it often has exciting finishes; and so on. Again this approach might work if I have for a long time been longing for these features in football, but if not, I might instead respond with all the reasons that I like football: it is an extreme physical challenge; it takes incredible courage just to take the field; and so on. We might then resort to a new approach: let's go to each other's games and get a taste for what it really feels like. This appears promising, but even if I understand what is going on at your game, if it doesn't touch what my heart longs for in a sport, it will still not appeal. The potential problem with all these approaches is that they only work if both you and I agree about what makes a sport good. Or to put it another way, the reasons you and I give for our sport being the best will only be convincing if you agree with the underlying value of what makes a sport best. If you think all violent

---

[2] 'Footy' and 'football' are names used of the Australian Rules Football game, a physical contact sport comparable with Rugby Football and American Football, though with fewer rules than the former and significantly less padding than the latter! (In this context it is important not to confuse it with Association Football or 'soccer').

contact is bad, and I think it can be brilliant as long as no-one gets badly hurt, how can we persuade each other to love our sport?

A creative solution to this dilemma might be for me to try to explain to you how my sport fits your idea of 'best'. So I could perhaps work out a way of explaining how football really isn't that rough (this could be tricky), or perhaps try to get you to like touch football instead. Perhaps I might secretly think that if you could first like touch football, you might then come to love tackle football! However this approach is unlikely to work because it lacks real integrity. It either forces each of us to compromise what we love, or to trick each other. In the end, if we both love our sports deeply then the only way to persuade each other to change our allegiance is for us to begin a much longer road of exploring what it is that makes a sport the best in the first place.[3]

This sport illustration gives a window into most of the current approaches to witnessing to Muslims. Some people (often called the polemicists) like to point out all the problems with Islam. This approach can work with dissatisfied Muslims but often leads to arguments that miss the mark in ways I have described earlier (Deedat). Others (often called the eirenicists) like to avoid criticism of Islam and aim to simply love Muslims and point out all the good things about Christianity. This is less likely to lead to arguments, but only works where people are already at the point where they are valuing the things Christianity has to offer as a religion. Some (the contextualisers) attempt to explain Christianity in Muslim terms. There are many different approaches to this, but they are often very complicated and require you to know Islam very deeply for it to work

---

[3] Now you might respond that the above illustration works for sport because the issue is about *taste*, not *truth*. There is no 'best' sport, you might say, no 'right' or 'wrong' sport to follow. You might say that questions about God are different because it is about *truth*. And you'd be right. But truth about God is not simple truth. The reasons we have for believing what we believe about God are complicated because (as we have seen) belief is complicated. And the reasons we have for choosing which reasons we value most are never completely objective because (as we have seen) we are influenced by our culture.

well. Worse, it can often result in a very poor version of Christianity which has had key parts taken out (like Jesus is the Son of God) or watered down to fit a Muslim world view.

Now don't get me wrong, I am not saying these approaches are necessarily bad. In fact, all these approaches are of value and can be found in the Bible. Jesus often used polemics to expose people's wrong assumptions (e.g. Mark 7:1-13). The invitation to come and find the excellent things we have found in Christianity is witnessed as early as the first disciples (John 1:35-51) and the man born blind (John 9). Paul is seen contextualising his message when he preached in Athens (Acts 17:16-34). But in all these cases, people were witnessing to others who had a similar world view to them, or again to people who had similar ideas of what was the best. This means they could start the conversation knowing that they understood where the other person was coming from.

Most of the time in witnessing to Muslims we need to be slow to make this assumption. Usually (as we have seen) we need to spend a long time first understanding where they are coming from. Then we will usually come to realise that they are coming from a very different place in what they value as the best when it comes to God, revelation, holiness and piety. We need to be prepared to take the longer road of exploring what is the best in all the things that make up people's beliefs. We might need to explore what makes a reliable authority, or what is intellectually best. We might need to explore what the best experience of God might be like, or what really makes life work. It is only when Muslims are wondering about these things, that they are open to hearing how Christ might answer their questions in a radically different way from any they have thought about. Again, it is only when Muslims are starting to ask these questions that polemics, eirenics, or appropriate contextualisation starts to touch their hearts.

As I finish this chapter it is important that you do not misunderstand my call to do some hard thinking as a lack of confidence in the gospel. As Christians we have great confidence that the gospel has the power to touch hearts (Romans 1:16), and that the Holy Spirit is at work preparing people to receive Christ (John 3:8,

WITNESSING TO WESTERN MUSLIMS

14). There is every chance that you may come across a Muslim whom God has prepared (often with a dream or vision) and whose heart is longing and ready to receive the gospel willingly. My experience, however, is that usually you will need to take the longer road of exploring deep questions of life with Muslims. This takes time. It takes effort. It takes love. It is sometimes fraught with frustration and misunderstandings. It takes doing life together. But that is our call. That is what it means to be witnesses (1 Peter 2:12).

I hope you are left wondering what all this looks like in practice, because that it what constitutes the rest of this book. It is an attempt to explore what Western Muslims believe, how to share life with them in a way that opens opportunities to display Christian holiness in ways Muslims will recognize, as well as ways of speaking the gospel that are most likely to be persuasive.

KEY POINTS:

o   *People are complicated, and the reasons people have for believing what they believe are also complicated.*

o   *Muslims generally have a different way of evaluating beliefs about God. This is partly because of what Islam values and teaches, and partly cultural.*

o   *Christians seeking to witness Christ to Muslims need to work hard at understanding where Muslims are coming from and then give reasons for Christian faith that touch Muslim hearts.*

---

2.   Believing...

"King Agrippa, do you believe the prophets? I know that you believe."

And Agrippa said to Paul, "In a short time would you persuade me to be a Christian?"

And Paul said, "Whether short or long, I would to God that not only you but also all who hear me this day might become such as I am"

Acts 26:27-29

Paul's witness to Christ before King Agrippa started with Paul asking himself a key question: "What does Agrippa already believe about God?" The answer to this question allowed Paul to speak truth in a way that Agrippa could engage with meaningfully. In the same way, we have just seen that in the encounter with Muslims, it is important to understand how Muslims come to believe what they believe. It is also important to know exactly what it is that Muslims believe about some key things. These key things include the basic beliefs of Islam and the basic practices of Islam. This is "Islam 101" sort of stuff and there are plenty of places you can find it, so I will not be detailing it here.[4] There are, however, some key beliefs Muslims have that that are not usually found in "Islam 101", but which have a huge impact

---

[4]   In summary, the five basic practices of Islam are: professing faith, praying five times a day, fasting (particularly during the month of Ramadan), giving to charity and going on pilgrimage to Mecca at least once if possible. The key beliefs of Muslims are in: Allah, the oneness of Allah, Prophets, Revealed books and angels. For a brief introduction check out *A Spectators Guide to World Religions* by John Dickson (Blue Bottle Books, Sydney, Australia 2004). For detailed Muslim teaching try islam.com, or islamworld.net. To drink from a fire hydrant regarding serious polemical arguments from both Christians and Muslims go to the Christian site www.answering-islam.org and the Muslim response www.answering-christianity.com

on encounters with Christians. They involve what Muslims believe about Christianity, particularly concerning what we hold in common, and what we believe differently. In order to speak to Muslims about Christ, like Paul, we need to know what these beliefs are.

On the other hand we must also look at some key beliefs that we have as Christians; both Christian beliefs we need to remember in the encounter with Islam and also beliefs Christians have about Islam. As we will see, both Muslims and Christians might be surprised by the inaccuracy of what we believe about each other's beliefs. Even if you are not surprised, the following beliefs are worth having in mind as you share with your Muslim neighbours so you can accurately say: "I know that you believe..."

2.1. Some things only Christians believe

There are two beliefs that Christians seeking to witness to Muslims need to cling tightly to. This is partly because they are at the very centre of what makes the Christian gospel different from any other faith, and partly because they are strongly denied in Islam, and easy to lose sight of when sharing with Muslims.

2.1.1. All humans are profoundly sinful

The Biblical idea of original sin found in the Bible is hard to explain, but crucial to believe. We need to remember it because, if we are willing to look deeply into our individual and corporate failure, it makes the most sense of the human experience. We also need to remember it because it points to the conspicuous inability of human religion to solve any of the deep issues faced by human failures throughout history (Colossians 2:20-23). It points to the need for transformation as fundamentally a heart matter, not an ideological matter. Most importantly, it points to the need for divine action rather than human action.

Islam clings tenaciously to the belief that, as humans, we are not only morally responsible for our own actions, but that if we obey God's guidance (the *sharia*) we are completely capable of living good lives, and creating just (Muslim) societies. As Muslim scholar

18

Shabbir Akhtar says: "...Muslims are religiously obliged to resist the tragic conclusion that man has failed in some ultimate and irreversible way".[5] Without a deep Christian conviction that this tragedy of the human sinful state is real, it will be difficult to resist the appeal of "religion", and to feel the urgency of the need of your neighbour to escape judgement. If, however, you hold your nerve on this conviction it can speak to the dilemma for Muslims that their denial of original sin doesn't seem to match real life. As Akhtar goes on to acknowledge: "...Muslims must, rightly or wrongly, refuse to concede the tragic failure of man, on pain of having no theology left to articulate." The Bible, on the other hand, has a lot of theology that articulates the human experience of sin.

2.1.2. *Jesus is the only saviour*

If humans are profoundly sinful and incapable of transforming ourselves, then it means we need outside help. We need God to come powerfully into our lives and to perform radical surgery on our hearts. We don't need simply to be good or obedient, we need to be born again (John 3). We don't simply need forgiveness for the times we are weak, we need a resurrection to new life. In short: we need a saviour.

My experience is that when sharing faith with Muslims it is easy to lose sight of the need for a saviour offering new life. You can quickly get bogged down in questions like: "If you are fully forgiven through the gospel, then why do you need to be good?" Or put another way: "If getting to heaven is all about what Jesus does, then why does what we do matter?" Now these are good theological questions, but you need to understand where they are coming from and why they are likely to be dead end conversations with Muslims. These questions are raised because for Muslims religion is essentially about *obedience*, not *salvation*. If you believe, like Muslims, that you *can* successfully be obedient, then of course you don't see the need for a saviour. Similarly, if you don't think you need a saviour then the gospel can easily be misread as simply a get-in-free ticket to heaven

---

[5]   Shabbir Akhtar, *A Faith for All Seasons*, Ivan Dee, Chicago, 1990. p161.

19

that bypasses obedience. We need constantly to remember that our bondage to sin demands a saviour, and that the name of Jesus is the only name by which people might be saved (Acts 2).

2.2. Some things only Muslims believe

2.2.1. The Qur'an and Sunna are obviously revelation

The Qur'an and the Sunna (the sayings and example of Muhammad) are for Muslims their only source of authoritative knowledge about God. It is important to realise that for most Muslims this is an unquestionable truth. While there are many recent Muslim publications that provide reasons, or evidence, for why the Qur'an is the word of God,[6] these are produced simply for the purpose of trying to convince a sceptical Western audience, not because most Muslims seek such evidence. Rather, for a Muslim the truth of Qur'an and Sunna is self evident in the same way that the existence of the universe obviously points to a creator, the existence of the Qur'an obviously points to the prophet-hood of Muhammad. Now as Christians we can seriously question the validity of this. We can ask questions of whether the Qur'an is a reliable text, or Muhammad is a reliable witness, or whether the Qur'an sourced its material from other traditions. But we need to know that Muslims for the most part will not practice, or enjoy, such questioning. Not only that, they will also usually have no answers to these questions, except to give you one of the publications I mentioned.

2.2.2. Islam is the "seal"

One of the reasons Muslims don't tend to be challenged by the existence of other religions claiming to have rival "revelations" is because they understand Islam to be the "seal" over all religion. By this they mean that Islam was the original religion, and that all true prophets, in all religions, preached Islam one way or another. You might think that the existence of religious diversity might provide a

---

[6] e.g. www.islam-guide.com

problem for this view, but the differences between religions is explained away by the assertion that the current shape of religions is due to distortion of the original prophets' messages. So, under this understanding, Jesus preached the same Islam as Muhammad but subsequent generations of Christians distorted the message into what now is found in the Bible. In Islam the job of Muhammad was to come and once for all put an end to distortions with a final, authoritative clarification of what all religions were actually on about – the Qur'an.

Now clearly this is a fairly imperialistic view. It means that Muslims say things like "we love Jesus", but that it is the Qur'anic version of Jesus they love, not the Biblical version. Similarly they say that they love the laws given to Moses, but again this means they love the Muslim understanding of them. Or, again, Muslims say that they believe in the gospel (the *injeel*), but that the only true gospel left is the Gospel of Barnabas.[7] For Muslims, if the Christian Bible agrees at all with the Qur'an it is because it has retained some truth from the original Islamic Bible, however if it disagrees it is because it has distorted Islam. The important point to realise is that if the Qur'an is the "seal" of all religions it means that Muslims can incorporate *any* different faith into Islam without having to actually look carefully at their claims.

2.2.3. Christians are...?

Relationships between Christians and Muslims can be complicated in Muslim communities largely because it is theologically complicated in Islam. Depending on what verses in the Qur'an you focus on (and how you interpret them) Christians can be friends or enemies, people of faith or people led astray, cousins or servants. How this works out in practice is that some Muslims will not want to befriend you, and

---

[7] Historians universally regard this to be a false gospel probably written by Muslims in the middle Ages. There are no texts of the document in existence, or even references to it in other texts, earlier than the 16th Century. Many of the details it mentions are clearly unhistorical.

some will. Some will see you as a believer who God accepts (although with some wrong beliefs), while others will see you as a *kaffir* – a spiritually unclean unbeliever.

My experience in ministry is that most Muslims will at least accept service from Christians. Sometimes this is because they think that God put Christians on earth to serve. Sometimes this is because in their understanding our pleasing of God is linked to the number of good works we do, so if they let Christians do some good works of service then they are doing us a favour by helping us build up brownie points! I have noticed that this can sometimes lead to Christians feeling that their efforts to love are rebutted, taken for granted, or even abused, but Christians should not be put off ministry by this misreading of our service. Jesus' service of humanity on the cross was profoundly misread and abused by many. He did not, however, stand up for his rights, or try to correct, he simply continued graciously to serve the undeserving (Isaiah 53, Romans 5:1-10). For grace truly to be grace it must be open to abuse. On the positive side, my experience is that for all the negative experiences, there are many Muslims who will simply see Christians as other believers who are willing to befriend them when many others won't. This is particularly true for refugees, or women in conservative Muslim communities who are often subject to public abuse.

2.3.   Some beliefs Muslims think Christians share with them (but Christians don't)

There is a strange dynamic in Muslim faith that on the one hand makes a lot out of the superiority of Islam, but on the other tries to make a strong case that it is exactly the same as Judaism and Christianity in key areas. This means that most Muslims I know genuinely think that I will believe the same as them about those key areas. Here are three of those issues, and, as we will see, there are, in fact, significant differences in what we believe.

2.3.1.   A prophet is someone who...?

Islam claims to be a prophetic religion. It believes that God has guided through the message and example of prophets throughout history. I have already mentioned that theologically this includes prophets of all religions, but in practice the Qur'an really only mentions some of the characters from the Bible. These include Adam, Moses, Job, David, Jonah and of course Jesus. Muslims believe that because they regard these Biblical figures as prophets that Islam stands very strongly in the Biblical prophetic tradition. They particularly believe that Christians will agree with them on who the prophets were and what their basic message was. The only substantial difference they see between Christianity and Islam regarding prophecy is the failure of Christians to acknowledge Muhammad as the last in the line of prophecy.

Christians, however, hold a very different view from Muslims on both the nature and message of the Biblical prophets. The first difference concerns the *role* of a prophet. In Islam a prophet is not just someone who speaks God's word, they are also great *examples* of faith. You might have noticed this in the fact that most of the people I just mentioned as Muslim prophets are not formally regarded in the Bible as 'prophets' in the way that someone like Isaiah might be. Instead they are kings and leaders and family heads. This is not a problem for Islam because Islam does not distinguish between the role of leadership and the role of prophecy in the way the Bible does. Muhammad performs the role of both Moses and Aaron, but is called a prophet. Again this is because the Qur'an points to these prophets as *examples* of faith, rather than recording what they actually said (this is especially true of Jesus). In fact Islam claims to have 70 000 prophets like this. This idea of prophets being exemplars is important to grasp because it means that Muslims expect prophets to live exemplary lives: a prophet could not possibly commit serious sin.

This is very different from the Bible where many of the key leaders and prophets had serious flaws and failures: King David being the classic example. As a result Muslims tend to use this as evidence that the Bible's accounts of these people must have been tampered with.

The second difference concerns message content. Unsurprisingly Muslims believe all prophets preached pure Islam.

Perhaps more surprisingly there is very little preaching content found in the Qur'anic stories concerning the prophets. Certainly no Muslim I have met is familiar with their message or context. One young Muslim I know was wearing a t-shirt that said "I love Jesus because I am a Muslim – and he was too!" When I asked him what he loved in particular about the things Jesus said he smiled and confessed that he knew nothing of what Jesus had actually said, but that it was a free t-shirt! Christians, however, can point to the messages of the prophets in the Bible bearing very little resemblance to Muhammad's message. Sure, they proclaimed (like Muhammad) that the one true God deserved worship, but they also spoke of worship being based in a covenant of grace not law, of once for all sacrificial atonement, of suffering servant Messiahs, of God turning up to shepherd his people, and of laws being written not in books but on hearts. None of this is found in the message of Muhammad.

2.3.2. We both believe in the Torah and the gospels

Pretty much everything I have just said about prophets could be applied to the Muslim view of the Torah (the first five books of the Old Testament) and the gospels. The Qur'an mentions them, and also the Psalms (called *Zabur*), as holy books confirming the message of Islam. Once again they are referred to by name, rather than content. Once again they are only seen of value if anything they contain aligns with the Qur'an. If it doesn't, it is because they have been changed. Finally, once again most Muslims will have little awareness of their content.

2.3.3. Islam is one of the three Abrahamic faiths

Muslims don't just want to claim to stand in the prophetic tradition of Judaism and Christianity, they also want to claim a genetic, and thus covenantal, link. They believe that the Arab people in general, and Muhammad in particular, are directly descended from Abraham's first son Ishmael (who is a legitimate son of Abraham in Islam). There is no real way of establishing the historical truth of this claim one way or the other, but in any case the point here is theological. They believe that as the eldest son, Ishmael inherited all the covenant

24

promises made to Abraham. If this is the case, then Muslims are legitimately part of God's chosen people, and therefore standing in line for a prophetic witness. In other words this belief is a claim to covenant legitimacy: "We are in the Abrahamic covenant club too!"

An interesting thing about this belief is that many well meaning Christians have bought into this language of late. This is unhelpful because it ignores the fact that Christianity doesn't hold Islam to be a theologically Abrahamic faith in the way Muslims do. The whole point of the Biblical Isaac/Ishmael story is that Ishmael was an *illegitimate* son, conceived by Abraham through doubt, not faith, and so Ishmael was never a bearer of the covenant. It was only Isaac who was the promise bearer, precisely because the covenant was just that: a promise through election. So whether Muhammad was descended from Abraham is beside the point: there is only one Abrahamic faith and it is faith in the covenant promises of God that culminate in Christ. This is not just cheap theological point scoring – it is not "Nah, nah, we are the real Abrahamic faith and you are not!" This is important because it hits on the key to Abrahamic faith always being covenant grace, not genetics or successful legal obedience.

2.4. Some things Muslims think Christians believe (but Christians don't)

By now you will realise that there are some significant differences in belief between Muslims and Christians. This is tricky enough if you want to talk about faith, but it is made trickier when Muslims criticise some Christian beliefs when they don't really understand them.

2.4.1. All Westerners are Christians

The standard historical Muslim argument goes like this: Nearly all Westerners are Christians, the West is immoral, therefore Christians are immoral. I would like to able to say that this Muslim belief is a superficial stereotype that Muslims who live in the West have realised is not true. And certainly there are many Western Muslims who see the difference between born again Christians and nominal Christians. However Muslims usually still think differently about this. In most Muslim communities if you are born Muslim you are always Muslim. Likewise if you are Somali you are Muslim, if you are Saudi Arabian you are Muslim etc. You might be a good Muslim or you might be a bad Muslim, but you *are* a Muslim. This is nominalism in the true sense of the word: my name/identity is "Muslim".

It is therefore natural for Muslims to see any person or culture with a Christian heritage as similarly Christian. They will then judge the behaviour of any supposed "Christian" by how they measure up morally, and thus judge them as either good or bad Christians. That is, they naturally apply their theology of obedience to Christianity. So, for example, I was once asked by a Muslim who the good Christian women they had seen in Australia were. When I asked which women they meant, I worked out they were talking about nuns. The nuns were good Christians because they covered their heads. Please don't think that this means that Muslims are not concerned with the state of people's hearts before God. They are. A good Muslim is supposed to love God with his or her heart. It is just that the test of such love is obedience to the path laid out in the *sharia*.

Here, it is important to remember that there is no such thing as a good or a bad Christian. Depending on how you want to say it there are: born again Christians or nominal Christians, Spirit filled Christians or un-regenerated unbelievers, real Christians or fake Christians, sheep or goats. Real Christians are bad people who have asked God to come into their lives and transform them from the inside out by His Spirit. What we do matters (as we will see in the next section), but the test of our faith will not be how successful we have been in our obedience.

Viewing all Westerners as Christians is not simply a theological issue concerning belief. It is also a political and tribal issue that touches on deep questions of both allegiance and justice. Many Muslims perceive the world in terms of the Muslim community (the *umma*) and the rest. There is a very strong belief that the Muslim community has historically been dealt a very rough hand by the international community in general, and Western political and business interests in particular. Much of this stems from the political impositions of the colonial period in the Middle East and Indian subcontinent. More recent events such as the establishment of, and subsequent conflict with, the state of Israel and ongoing wars in the Persian Gulf and Afghanistan also contribute to this belief. All such events are perceived as unjust oppressions of the *umma* undertaken by a Christian West, out of political or economic self interest. To make matters worse for Christian witness, much of the missionary effort of the church to the Muslim world in the past has been understood as riding on the back of such Western imperialism, and in fairness there is some truth to this. There are many instances of well intentioned, yet culture bound missionaries who carry more than just the gospel into the Muslim world.

Whatever the accuracy of this common Muslim understanding of history, it is important not to underestimate the depth of feeling around these issues. "Us and them" is a dynamic that can drive all of us powerfully. In the Olympic Games some of my favourite events are the middle distance running races. In these races I have to confess to always hoping for the Kenyan "Christians" to beat the Algerian or Ethiopian "Muslims". I justify this on the basis of being married to a wife who was born and grew up in Kenya! But if I am honest there is more going on for me: deep down I want my Christian side to succeed over the Muslim side. At the Olympics such tribalism can be fun, but in the real world it has often been deadly. This means that even though Western Muslims might love their country of residence, they may still, deep down, support their Muslim 'tribe' even more. This may mean, for example, that issues around Muslim terrorism are complicated for them. Western Muslims may be against terrorism as a solution to injustice, but still have a deep sympathy for the cause that terrorists are pursuing. All this means that not only must Christians witnessing to Muslims be clear in distinguishing between nominal and born again faith, we must also be clear in distinguishing between Western imperialism, and the true Kingdom of Heaven. In line with this we must display a passion for the Biblical call both to seek justice and to love even our enemies.

2.4.2. What we do doesn't matter

Because Muslims understand faith in terms of being good or bad, when they hear a Christian explain the gospel of grace, their usual reaction is that if forgiveness is completely to do with what Jesus did, then our actions, whether sinful or obedient, do not matter. The thinking goes like this: if forgiveness is freely available simply by having faith in Christ, then what stops Christians from keeping on sinning knowing that they will be forgiven? Another way I have heard Muslims express this to me is: are you saying that if Hitler believed in Jesus then he would be in heaven? To the Muslim mind the gospel suggests that forgiveness is cheap, that laws will be ignored and that obedience is devalued.

To be fair this is a good question. The Book of Romans spends a couple of chapters wrestling with the same question, with Paul asking "What then? Shall we sin because we are not under law but under grace?" (Romans 6:15). This makes sense because the early church was very Jewish and, like Islam, heavily concerned with questions of obedience to law. The way the Book of Romans addresses this question reinforces the distinctiveness of the gospel message: the only pathway to obedience is through dying and being born again as a new person, with a new heart which has God's laws written on it. Christians are people whose hearts long for God and his Kingdom life. Christians choose obedience because we were not just forgiven for sin, but we "died to sin" (Romans 6:8-10).

A great illustration of this is found in the testimony of a Brazilian man I know. As a young man he had no interest in God and was into drugs and gangs. One day he was passing by a church that met in a cinema, and without any clear idea why, he wandered in and sat down at the back. During the pastor's message he sat there thinking how stupid the gospel was. However, when the pastor made an appeal to come to faith, the young man found himself praying the prayer! As he described it, the Holy Spirit entered his life at that point and he walked out a believer. A little while later he was in the bush near his town when two friends from his gang life rode past on horses and invited him to share some drugs they had just purchased.

He said to them, "The person you knew is now dead. The person you see now is a new person in Christ and doesn't do drugs anymore. And if you try and make him he will beat you up!" This is not just a funny story; it captures the essence of being Christian. After coming to faith Christians still have rough edges, God has lots of work to do in us, but we are new people. As I have said to Muslims many times, now that God is in my life, I don't *want* to live the old life I used to live.

2.4.3.   *Our sin is paid for by a 'third party'*

Because Muslims refuse to acknowledge that Jesus was God, they have a big problem with the crucifixion. If Jesus wasn't God then an innocent man is being punished, and this is obviously unjust. More than that, what has the suffering of an innocent man got to do with anyone else's sin? How can a third party take responsibility for my, or anyone else's, sin?

The cross of Christ presses two Muslim heresy buttons at once. First, the worst sin you can commit in Islam is *shirk*, which means worshipping or associating any thing with God (i.e. idolatry). Saying Jesus is God is *shirk* for Muslims. Second, in Islam humans are completely responsible for their own actions and must stand alone before God and give account for them. We have seen that Muslims are optimistic about this because they do not believe in original sin. This optimism, combined with God's demand to give a personal account, means that Muslims don't see the need for the cross: if I can be obedient then I do not need a saviour, and if I must answer to God then I do not need a substitute.

Because the gospel of atonement through a crucified Christ is unacceptable to Muslims, there is a temptation for Christians to downplay the divinity of Jesus. One example is the emergence in the mission world of new "contextualised" Bible translations for Muslims that remove any reference to Jesus as the "Son of God". I believe this to be a mistake. It is crucial to hold firmly to the divinity of Christ, otherwise the cross makes no sense. If Jesus was *not* God then Muslims are correct that Christians are idolaters, and the cross involves a third party suffering innocently, and in a way that is of no help to anyone. But if Jesus *was* actually God then worshipping him is not idolatry. And if Jesus *was* actually God then the cross is not a third party paying for sin, but is all about God forgiving our sin himself.

KEY POINTS:

o   *The key distinctive of the gospel of Christ is salvation from profound sinfulness, into a new life in the Spirit.*

o   *Most Muslims unquestioningly believe in the truth of Islam, and an Islamic understanding of all other faiths.*

o   *Muslims usually think they understand, and sometimes agree with, what Christians believe. Often, however, these are misunderstandings.*

---

3. Living...

"Keep your conduct among the Gentiles honourable, so that when they speak against you as evildoers, they may see your good deeds and glorify God on the day of visitation."

1 Peter 2:12

Christian witness is about displaying the difference that following Jesus makes to our lives. We do not simply claim to believe in Jesus, we claim that his Holy Spirit dwells in us and transforms us from glory to glory (2 Corinthians 3). We claim that He is changing us into people who live Godly lives – lives that are more and more like God everyday. But what does that look like? What is it about our lives that will stand out clearly and unambiguously as evidence of God's power at work? Sometimes it is a little unclear how people with different worldviews evaluate our witness. We might think we are witnessing, but according to a lot of the missionary books we might instead be offending!

3.1. Dos and Don'ts?

Many of the books that deal with relating to Muslims make a lot out of certain behaviours that might be misread and create misunderstanding or even offence. The usual candidates are expressed as a list of behavioural *dos* and *don'ts* and include things such as: don't put your Bible on the floor, do take off your shoes at the door, don't shake hands with someone of the opposite sex, do dress modestly, don't drink or offer alcohol, etc. I have learned the hard way that there as many such issues as there are Muslim cultures.

Every year in our ministry we run a summer camp at the beach. It is a great time of fun and relaxation, and our hope is that it displays the joy of Christian community to the campers, of whom the majority are Muslim. Camp culminates on the last night with a camp concert in which many campers perform different acts. Every year I do an act which involves dropping a swimming cap full of water onto a volunteer's head from a height. It is a great trick that the crowd loves as the cap miraculously sticks on the volunteers' head, and they get wet too. One year I thought it would be an even better trick to do it a second time with a capful not just of water, but cold soup from the kitchen, using my son as a prepared volunteer. In my imagination this was a great witness of how Christians have fun together. On the night, however, the Muslim audience was horrified. They asked me how on earth I could tip rubbish from the bin on my child? They even told me that they were praying for me that God would forgive me for treating my child like this. So much for pointing to Christ! Later over coffee I was able to assure them both that it was not rubbish, but clean food that my son was happy about, and also, that in any case, I was confident of my forgiveness by God because of Jesus.

Now what do we make of an incident like this? Clearly, I now recognize that tipping rubbish over your child is a 'don't' of Muslim ministry (in that cultural context at least!). I had obviously caused offence, or at least not acted in a way that clearly commended the excellence of Christianity to the Muslim audience. The question for me is: was this incident an example of good witness? I think it was (or at least it wasn't a complete disaster) and here is why. It is clear from this story that the witness of our lives is not always obvious without explanation. Our behaviour is always viewed through the culture and values of the watcher. But here is the thing: it is not one-off events that bear unambiguous witness to Christ. Instead the actions of our lives are explained to people through the context of our relationships with them. So, on camp any offence of mine was graciously overlooked because the Muslim audience already knew me and (hopefully) liked me – at least they liked me enough to pray for God to forgive me! In fact it was because they knew me, and had watched many of my actions in the past, that they were surprised I would do such a thing. But more than this, the fact that we were in relationship meant that I, and others, got the chance to talk deeply about the God issues involved. Any witnessing ambiguity caused by my actions was removed by speaking clearly of Christian hope for forgiveness. The witness of our lives builds as relationships deepen, and this is especially the case with neighbours, or work or play mates, who get to know us well!

I believe that in witnessing to Muslims there are no absolute dos and don'ts, except one: Do commit boldly and faithfully to share your Christ centred life with your Muslim neighbours or workmates or friends. This does not mean you should not try to be aware of how your actions are understood, nor that you should just be yourself and not modify your behaviour for the sake of your neighbour. It does mean however that we should not think it is all too hard because we don't get the cultural or religious rules. As one of my team members says: "...it's not rocket science, just sit down, have a cup of tea, and get to know people! They will tell you if something really offends them, and you can tell them why you do what you do." We need to remember here that in downplaying dos and don'ts, I am particularly talking about witnessing to Western Muslims. Muslims in the West might not completely understand Christianity, but they get the way that Western people live – and most of them live very similarly! They are used to reading the behaviour of the people around them, and they don't expect that everyone will act like them. (Having said this about Western Muslims, my experience of living in Muslim countries suggests that even there, most Muslims are very gracious and not at all precious about misunderstandings if they know you and trust you.) Most Muslims I know are not at all precious about this, and in fact cross-cultural and religious misunderstandings lead to laughter more often than they lead to offence!

If witness is as simple as just being Christian in your relationships with people, why not end the chapter here? Here's why. While I don't want to give you a list of dos and don'ts, I do want to address some of the tensions you will inevitably find yourself wrestling with in trying to provide a relevant Christian witness that goes beyond removing offence.

3.2.   Which do's and don'ts?

In 1 Corinthians 9 Paul talks about one of his key witnessing principles being this:

> ...though I am free and belong to no man, I make myself a slave to everyone, to win as many as possible. To the Jews I become like a Jew, to win the Jews...To the weak I became weak, in order to win the weak. I have become all things to all people so that by all possible means I might save some.

Now being "all things to all people" sounds like a nice idea, but in reality it is complicated. For a start, becoming all things is obviously not an absolute principle. I doubt Paul would become a thief to win thieves. 'All things' is limited by the morals of his faith. I doubt, too, whether Paul would have been willing to become a Muslim to win Muslims (although some Christians attempt this in both Western and Muslim countries!). That is because 'all things' is also limited by the theology of his faith. It is these limits that cause tension. The limits are set by the demand to live a holy life, a life of Christian integrity, where what we believe to be true and value deeply is reflected in our lives. The big question is: How far should I embody someone else's understanding of holiness in order to witness to them? This is not just a hypothetical question. In witnessing to Muslims you will need to decide on limits for yourself, as we have found.

For example, over the years in our ministry we have run many community barbeques. Due to the majority Muslim population we provide *halal* meat – that is, meat killed and prepared according to Islamic law. This means that many Muslims feel able to join in and eat with us. At the same time, it means that some from a Christian background have problems joining us, believing us to be serving meat sacrificed to idols. You might think it is a simple issue, but considering there is a whole chapter of the Book of Romans devoted to a similar issue (chapter 14 and into 15) perhaps it is a little more complicated.

Here are some of the issues involved. First, there are questions of how Muslims might view it: They may see it as us being nice and welcoming to them *or* they may see it as us being willing to compromise our own convictions due to the divine command to eat *halal* food, or even as us taking first steps to recognising the superiority of Islam. Second, there is the question of its Christian integrity. We might argue that idols are not real, so we are free to eat what we like. We might argue that we shouldn't do anything that causes fellow Christians to go against their conscience. We may avoid it on the basis that we are endorsing the authority of a false religion. We may be for it because it sends the message that Christ frees us from such concerns as food laws. It is complicated, and there are no right answers, only hopefully wise answers (you'll notice Paul doesn't give a 'right' answer, in Romans 14, on which way to go).

Now, as I mentioned, we have chosen in our context to share *halal* food with Muslims. Here is our thinking: It is OK because we believe it is no compromise to our faith to eat *halal* meat because idols are not real. It is OK because it is a testimony to our freedom in Christ to eat what we choose. It is OK because we value shared community meals, over the risk that Muslims might see it as us compromising our own faith. It is OK because (as good Aussies) we value having lots of real meat at a BBQ, over the option of vegetarian burgers (which would have no *halal* issues)! It is OK because it is an expression of love and welcome. Are we right? I'm not sure there is a right answer, but we have sat down, prayed, thought and tried to be wise in order to win some. You will need to ask the same questions if you invite your Muslim neighbour to a meal at your place. What would you decide?

Another example of this sort of tension is found in the issue of drinking alcohol, or eating pork. Many Christians drink alcohol. Many more eat pork, and especially bacon – even many Muslims I know don't think of bacon as pork because it tastes so good on pizza! Both alcohol and pork, however, are banned in Islam, and abstinence from them is one the key markers of religious purity or holiness for Muslims. As a Christian how should you handle alcohol or pork if you want to witness to Muslims? At the very least it seems wise to avoid offering Muslims pork or alcohol, but is that enough? Should you, too, abstain from pork or alcohol when you are around Muslims?

Should you maybe abstain completely from them as a good witness, so you can be obviously leading a pure and holy life? Or should you refuse to abstain to witness freedom in Christ? What does it mean to be all things here? How will you decide? So far I have given two examples of issues where it is complicated choosing how to act as a good witness, but there are many others involving things like: the roles of men and women in community events and worship, styles of worship and religious teaching, styles of celebration and community events, and the exercise of community discipline and authority models.

If there was one issue, however, that goes close to being a clear 'do', it is this: do any personal witness within your own gender. That is, males should witness to males and females should witness to females. There are many reasons for this. Mostly it is because this is usually culturally appropriate. In conservative Muslim communities men and women who are not family may only mix in public for business or educational reasons. Even in more liberal Muslim cultures where men and women mix freely in work or socially, it will still be generally permitted only as a group activity. Another reason is that, at the risk of gross generalisation, Muslim women and men tend to have different approaches to their faith. This varies with the communities, but women tend to visit the mosque less, and have more of a traditional and practical (but often stronger) folk Islam. Connecting with such women will generally involve visiting them in their homes, and spending many hours drinking tea and coffee with them and their friends and relatives. On the other hand, men, especially if they bother to go to the Mosque regularly, will tend to be more formally taught, and enjoy arguing theology more. To connect deeply with men in Muslim communities usually will involve going to the places they socialise, like coffee shops, restaurants or basketball courts. (A possible exception to this is university groups where there are increasing numbers of educated, articulate and activist Muslim women). There are darker reasons too for keeping witness gender specific. Sadly there are many Muslim men who, while often charming, have a poor view of Western women, and will expect them to be sexually available. Moreover, for a few evangelistically minded

Muslim men, marrying Christian women is seen as a valid strategy to grow Islam, and they will actively pursue them.

But it is not just for these reasons that men should witness to men, and women to women. It is also for our Christian reputation. Ephesians 5:3 warns us that there should not be even a hint of sexual immorality in the Christian community. Muslim communities generally view Westerners to be universally sexually immoral. And from even a brief glance at our television, movies, nightlife or university campus life it is hard not to agree with them! As Christians, though, we must be above reproach. There is irony here. Behind the genuine public concern for sexual purity, it is common in Islam for there to be a profound sexualisation of all male/female relationships. All non-family male/female relationships are assumed to be sexual. (Over the years I have been introduced to many "cousins" when I have run into a Muslim friend and he has been alone with a girl). But as Christians we must witness in a way that shows we are not captive to sexual desires. In the end this too is not simply a do or a don't but is another example of witnessing by living a holy life.

All these issues are important to wrestle with, particularly if you are in a role of Christian leadership, but again a warning is helpful here. Be prayerfully intentional about these things, but don't over-think this stuff! I have already mentioned that Western Muslims don't tend to be too precious about them. I also have a suspicion that Christians are far more fussed about this sort of thing than all but the strictest Muslims. I have Muslim friends who buy me Scotch whiskey as presents (even though I don't drink it!), I have been in after sport contexts where I have been the only one to abstain while my Muslim friends drank beer. I have helped run events with Muslim youth workers who ordered Pizza Hut pizza and then told the kids it was *halal.* I have been told to hold towels up as a modesty shield at the beach while Muslim women have stripped and changed in front of me! I have tried to take my shoes off, and been ordered not to because it is not my culture to. Again relationships and the Western context are keys. Western Muslims already make compromises, and even those who don't adopt the Western culture, don't expect you to be

WITNESSING TO WESTERN MUSLIMS

completely like them. And where tensions do occur, relationships allow them to be addressed, often leading to great conversations about faith!

3.3. Saints or sinners?

By now you may have picked up that there is a lot more going on here than just do's and don'ts. The whole idea of our actions being a witness hinges on us living holy lives – that is, lives set apart for God. The problem is that different people have different ideas of what holiness is and what it looks like. I believe that the key issue here is about what a holy person, or a holy life, looks like. As a general rule Muslims will view holiness similarly to the way the Pharisees did in the Bible. A holy person will be someone who faithfully keeps all God's rules and regulations. Particularly, they will pray and fast at all the appointed times, they will give to the poor, and make pilgrimage. They will follow the example of Muhammad. They will seek to be *halal* – only doing what is permitted by God – in all things. The Mosque will be the centre of their lives. Not only this, they will do all this carrying a religious demeanour. This means that they will be serious, not frivolous. They will avoid trivial things like TV, music, movies and sport. They will live simple lives, with few possessions. They will dress and groom like Muhammad. They will walk, not run. Very few Muslims I have met will claim to be such a holy person, however those in the Muslim community who are seen to be holy like this are held in high esteem – even by bad Muslims.

Now this is a problem for Christian witness. We want to witness by holy lives, but our lives usually don't look anything like the life of a Muslim holy person. Not only that, we don't want them to! We want to be serious about our faith, but we want to be joyful people too. We want to enjoy appropriately all God's good gifts, not to be ascetics who abstain by rule. We want to be culturally creative people, not people who emulate the example of a seventh century Arab man. We want to be people who love the lost, not people who avoid unclean "baddies". To many Muslims this does not equate to a holy life. A while ago I heard a young Aussie man who converted to Islam give his testimony at a large Muslim meeting. He talked about how as a youth he had gone along to some Christian camps, but how he couldn't get why the Christians were always singing? He lamented that instead of taking God seriously, the Christians were treating religion like a party. As he spoke the whole Muslim audience was clapping in affirmation. The dilemma is that, for Christians, our joy in Christ is profoundly holy. In fact it is one of the great blessings we hold out in the gospel. Should we stop singing to look holy to Muslims? Again this is not a hypothetical question. Personally speaking I feel this dilemma profoundly because as a church leader, and religious teacher, I am expected to be just such a holy person.

How then should we decide on how to act in order to display a holy life? My suggestion, and what I attempt to do, is to act in such a way that you are accused of what Jesus was accused of. When we look at Jesus' life we see that the Pharisees, in particular, had trouble working him out. He was presenting himself as a religious teacher, but his behaviour and demeanour was not at all like that which a holy person was expected to show. He was condemned as unholy for ignoring religious laws for the sake of helping people. He was condemned as unholy for hanging around with sinners and unclean people. He was condemned as unholy for partying. At the same time he practiced extreme spiritual disciplines (for example, fasting for 40 days) and his teaching was challenged for setting standards of living and pleasing God, that were too high! However I live, whatever I choose to do or not do, I want to be seen the same way. I want to be seen as someone who values love and service over rules, but I also want to be seen as someone who sets profoundly high moral standards. I want to be seen partying, and I want to be seen praying in all sorts of weird situations. I want our team to be seen as people passionate about God, but I want our Christian community to be open to all sorts of broken, unclean, and unholy people who want to find Him. In short, my hope is that all Christians witnessing to Muslims can say with Paul: "Follow my example, as I follow the example of Christ." (1 Corinthians 11:1)

For me it looks something like this. As we were departing for a community camp, a young man turned up at the bus wanting to come along. He was well known around our Estate as a drug user, yet he had turned up claiming he had been clean for months and now wanted to turn his life around through inviting God into his life and joining God's people. The Muslims who were coming on camp were asking why on earth we were letting someone like him – in other words a bad person – come along? To be honest I was asking myself the same thing later that day, as the kid was going through withdrawal (he turned out not to be as clean as he claimed!). I was still asking myself why I had said yes at three in the morning as I was driving for many hours back into the city to take him home. Now you might think that after many years of inner city ministry we would not do something stupid like let kids like this come along, and I did feel a little stupid. And you also might think that this would have resulted in an "I told you so" response from the Muslim campers, and I am sure there were some who thought that. At the same time, however, a number of the Muslims were highly impressed by the way our whole team cared for the young man while he was there. And some were completely blown away by the thought that some of our team would lose a night's sleep to do it. In the end, the thing for me was that, whatever anyone else thought of the incident, I was proud of our team because it seemed like the sort of crazy act of holy grace that Jesus might be involved in.

3.4.   Bold grace?

So far the point on holiness is that Christians should be holy by Jesus' grace standards, not Islam's *sharia* standards. However I need to clarify a possible misunderstanding. Christians witnessing to Muslims must not think that being people of grace means just being nice or polite or helpful or timid or refusing to debate truth. Similarly Christians must not think that serving Muslims means being doormats or people who never say no. You can be a grace person and be very bold. You can be a grace person who tells people things they don't want to hear. In fact not only can we be bold and gracious, we must be. Again look at Jesus. He was full of grace and truth (John 1). He touched lepers and welcomed children and yet he also called people snakes and dogs.

Now Christians need to be very careful in how we are bold

with Muslims. As a part of our holy lives our boldness must be on Jesus' terms, but there is the temptation to play by Islam's rules here. Islam is an "enforced" faith. I don't mean by this that Muslims are all unwillingly forced to be Muslim, or that all Muslims are *jihadists* trying to force Islam onto Australia, but traditional Islam demands obedience to God's law. This involves personally submitting to that law – that is the definition of the word Muslim: one who submits. But more than that, Islam involves seeking to impose God's laws on every situation in family and Muslim community life (for the sake of the community). As a result community and legal pressure is very powerful in Muslim families and Muslim communities. Leaving Islam is often dealt with severely (even in Western countries people's lives can be in danger if they leave conservative communities), as it is seen as damaging not only the individual, but also the community. Most Muslims will regard some degree of enforcement of Islam as a good thing. They will often think along the lines that if faith involves community allegiance and obedience, and if some ignorant people don't know what's best for themselves, then community pressure/enforcement at some level is appropriate. This sort of pressure may even be used on non-Muslims in attempts to convert them to Islam, as we have experienced.

At one of our community events a Christian girl from our team was with a group of Muslim girls. They were mucking around with fashion accessories and at one point she put a scarf on her head. The Muslims girls saw this as an opportunity for conversion, saying that she looked great as a Muslim. The group then surrounded her and the praise turned quickly into pleas to convert, and then soon after, into demands and intense intimidation. This was seen as good pressure, applied for her sake – they did not want her to go to hell and would do anything to try to stop that happening! For them, peer pressure was seen as a valid form of persuasion. I am not suggesting that all Muslims would act like this in a similar situation, or that all Muslims will seek enforcement of Islam on the unwilling. It is important, though, to be aware of the tendency towards imposition in any essentially legislative worldview. This is not exclusive to Islam – there are plenty of churches that resort to legalism too – but it is a powerful human tendency common to Muslim communities.

As people of grace, however, Christians should not use any form of pressure or intimidation or manipulation or enforcement in witness – including using argument as a blunt force. We must, however, be *bold*. We must be bold because it is Biblical. We are called to be lights, and lights that are not covered, but shining on a hill (Matthew 5:14-15). We are people who call out to God to make us bold and do amazing things through us (Acts 4:23-31). We must be bold because it is culturally appropriate for Muslims. Muslims see faith as a public issue, so people should be publicly out there about their faith. More than that, they would read any reluctance to be bold about your beliefs as a faith weakness. We should be bold beyond what feels right in our contemporary Western culture. Most Western cultures value plurality, and shy away from rigorous critique of other people's deeply held beliefs (we call this political correctness). Most of us have this sort of politeness built into us in such a way that we will feel uncomfortable being boldly Christian – not wanting to cause offence. My hunch is, however, that most Christians tone down their boldness long before there is any chance of offending Muslims. Our danger is being seen as weak or embarrassed about our faith, rather than being seen as offensive Bible bashers.

What might such boldness, without pressure, look like? Here are some ideas.

3.4.1. It must look like a public faith

In a sense this whole chapter is about having a public faith but it is important, especially in new relationships with Muslims, to display publicly and obviously your Christian identity in various ways that Muslims recognise as signs of religious faith. In Egypt, many Coptic Christians wear cross tattoos, but you don't need to go to this extreme to be publicly Christian. Simple things might include always having a Bible prominent in your home, or hanging Christian posters or Bible verses on your walls. One guy I know makes sure he mentions that he is Christian in the first conversation he has with any Muslim. Sometimes I will wear a T-shirt with a Jesus theme or a Bible verse printed on it. Over time it is important to use God gossip: dropping

WITNESSING TO WESTERN MUSLIMS

things into conversations like "the other day at church..." or "this is so and so from my home group..." or by saying a prayer of thanks before a meal or a family gathering. Of course these things are all superficial unless they are backed up with a consistent Christian faith, but it is important to be seen to be boldly living under Christ's banner, and these are the sorts of signs that Muslims will recognise as pointing to Christian allegiance.

3.4.2.   It looks like bold praying

Look for any opportunity to pray for and with Muslims. Pray prayers of thanks, and pray prayers of petition. Pray for everyday boring stuff, and pray for miracles. Most Muslims will be more than happy for you to pray for them, including praying for them while you are with them (although they will rarely pray out loud in my experience). This is a powerful witness as Christian prayer is distinctive in its intimacy with God through the presence of the Holy Spirit. Always pray in Jesus' name, not because they are magic words, but because it is boldly declaring our faith. One of the Muslim people groups I have lived and worked with has a reputation for being among the toughest and most resistant to the gospel. There are only a tiny number of Christians from this group around the world, and perhaps only a handful of public believers in my country. One day a young man from this community asked me for a reference for a court case he was facing, in which he had already pleaded guilty. I provided the reference, but also asked him if we could pray. He agreed and we prayed in his doorway the day before the case. A few days later he called me to say that the judge had pardoned him, and that he was absolutely convinced that it was my prayer that had provided the great outcome. After this he was willing to take a Bible – the only man from this group who has taken one from me!

3.4.3.   It also looks like doing church boldly

Take every opportunity to welcome Muslims into Christian fellowship, whether it is church or gatherings in homes, or picnics or dinner parties or camps. Like prayer, Christian gatherings are very distinctive (hopefully!) in their thankfulness, joy, love and ministry to each other, study of God's word and their passion for God to transform our lives. In our ministry over the years we have had many cases of Muslims finding themselves in tears as a result of sitting in on Christian worship.

3.4.4. *Sometimes it can look like saying 'no' boldly*

This is tricky, and it is not about making rules, but you must refuse to compromise your faith. We have talked about modifying our behaviour and how some things, like food, don't matter and can make it easier to enjoy friendship with Muslims. Some things, however, do matter if they compromise your conscience. A friend of mine has a family member who married a Muslim. Whenever the in-laws come over to visit, they ask whether the women can stay out of the rooms in the house where the men are, including asking my friend to not eat with her husband, but separately. My friend chooses to say no because it sends the message that she will not compromise her faith on key things that she values as a Christian – like unity in Christ, and her home being under the banner of Christ's Lordship.

3.4.5. *Finally it looks like speaking boldly*

The content of our speech is so important I am dedicating the whole next chapter to it, but I want to give one illustration of how boldness is important in our gospel proclamation. A Christian friend of mine is well known for public debates with Muslims on university campuses worldwide. One of the dynamics they noticed in the debates was that the Muslims in the audience would chant loudly *"Allahu Akbar!"* (God is greater) before the debates started as a form of intimidation or ground claiming. One day one of the Christian groups decided to respond with similar chants of "Jesus is Lord!" You might expect that this would have led to heated tensions. Instead, what happened was that both groups chanted for a while until everyone recognised that the other group was just as passionate about their faith as they were so intimidation wasn't going to work. After this everyone settled down quietly to listen to the debate! What is the lesson here? I believe it would have been highly ungracious for the Christians to start the chanting in an attempt to intimidate the

Muslims. However, Christians can refuse to be intimidated. In that context, the call to boldness demanded that the Christians should take a public stand for Christ. We must not be scared always to live our lives clearly under Christ's banner.

3.5. The greatest...

Perhaps you are a bit overwhelmed (again!) that it all seems rather complicated. Maybe it seems too hard to know what it means to be all things to all people. Maybe making wise choices about how to live lives that look holy seems impossible. Maybe boldness is too scary. If that is you, then don't panic. Instead remember Jesus' promise in John 13:35. Jesus promised that it would be the love Christians had for each other (and our enemies!) that would point to the truth of the gospel. If everything I have said seems too hard, or even if it doesn't, cling on to that promise, because it is true. One of the constant refrains in testimonies of Christians who have come from Muslim backgrounds is that they were impressed, and even amazed, by the love of Christians. Sometimes it was that they were loved by Christians, sometimes they witnessed Christians loving others. Either way, love, as 1 Corinthians 13 says, is the greatest.

Here is one of those testimonies. A good friend of mine grew up Muslim, and was passionately concerned for the injustices in the Muslim world. He could see people, especially his own ethnic group, suffering, and he couldn't understand why all the rich Muslim countries were doing nothing about it. For a while he sought answers in radical Islamism, believing the problem to be that Muslim countries were not Muslim enough, but eventually he saw that radical Islamism didn't have the deep solutions he was looking for. Later he ended up studying in the West, and in his first year became sick. He was alone in a foreign country and the only person who cared deeply for him during this time was one of his academic supervisors. He saw in this lecturer something of the sort of unmerited compassionate concern that he had been searching after for years. So he asked the man why he cared, and the man answered simply that he was a Christian, and Christians loved like Jesus loved. My friend resolved to find out more about this Jesus and it led him down a road to faith. The lecturer's witness was profoundly simple. He had had little experience with Muslims and had considered very little of what I have written about in this book – but he loved. And love is the greatest.

Please do not take the lesson of this testimony to be that all I have been discussing in the book so far is useless as long as you are compassionate and loving! Believe me, your witnessing to Muslims (or anyone else for that matter) will be much more effective if you think hard about worldviews and beliefs, as well as how best to display holiness in a way that is not easily misread. In fact it takes deep love to put the effort into thinking about these things. But remembering Jesus' promise will remind you that even if you do some dumb or offensive things; even if you are too free, or too constrained, in the way you try to accommodate your Muslim neighbours; even if you are misunderstood in your attempts to be obviously Christian; even if you are too timid or too bold in your attempts to present Christ; that in the end the best witness is through faithful, persevering, and caring relationships.

KEY POINTS:

o   *Be committed to live a life of bold Christian integrity.*

o   *Be culturally appropriate where possible, use your freedom in Christ wisely, but always be people of grace.*

o   *Be committed to faithful, loving, serving relationships.*

4. Talking...

"Always be prepared to give an answer to everyone who asks you to give the reason for the hope that you have. But do this with gentleness and respect..."

1 Peter 3:15

4.1. Evangelistic inadequacy

Some Christians are supremely gifted evangelists; most are not. A few people I have worked with in ministry have been able quickly and easily to share Christ with Muslims in a way that has seen immediate fruit. I know an Arab Christian who lives in the Middle East and who wanders the streets simply talking to Muslim people about Jesus. He usually sees at least one person put their faith in Christ every time he goes out! I know another Christian who is similarly gifted in the West. A while ago I went along with him to a Muslim public meeting at a local university. He and I were among only a few Christians who were there to hear the speaker (a Western convert to Islam) and maybe to ask some questions. During a break in the meeting the few Christians scattered around the room were surrounded by groups of Muslims engaging us in good natured, but spirited, debates about faith. I ended up with a few people wanting my email address, but later didn't hear back from any of them. My friend ended up with a number of people who wanted to continue to meet with him to read the Bible together. These two people are examples of gifted evangelists. I suspect they don't need to read a book like this because either they just naturally get the stuff I'm talking about, or God uses them to witness anyway (probably both!).

Most of us, however, are not gifted like these people, even if we want to be. Most Christians are not outstanding natural evangelists except perhaps for the first few months of our faith until we realise that perhaps not everyone else is as excited about Jesus as we are. Most of us are not missionaries or pastors who get to practice evangelism all the time. Most of us do not go out chasing opportunities to debate with Muslims at mosques or universities. On the contrary, we find ourselves in conversations about faith that we are neither looking for nor feel prepared for. More than that, most Christians I know who try to speak to Muslims about Jesus get into discussions they get confused by. Most feel they gave poor reasons for their faith, or didn't have good answers for the questions they were asked. Most have thought of a better thing to say long after the conversation was over. Some, myself included, have said things they regretted later. All this adds up to most Christians I know feeling evangelistically inadequate a lot of the time.

I suspect that part of the problem of feeling inadequate also comes from a longing to have an evangelistic "lay down misere" – an unbeatable case for faith in Christ.[8] By this I mean that in each evangelistic conversation we want to be able to present an irresistible testimony to the power of Jesus in our lives, or argue a knock down proof of the truth of Christianity, or deal a devastating killer blow to the truth of Islam (or any other faith). This is particularly true for someone who likes getting into (and winning!) debates. But even if we are not argumentative by nature, we want to be persuasive! We want people to encounter the gospel message in a powerful way that leads them to give their life to it. However, my experience of talking with Muslims (and anyone else) is that most of the time, there are no knockout blows either way, and that conversations get complicated and frustrating.

One traditional solution to evangelistic inadequacy is for Christians to use tracts. In this context I include in that category both booklets and memorized gospel presentations, sometimes using diagrams, and usually using Scripture references. There are a number of such tracts available that are designed to present Christ to Muslims in a way that helps them to understand the gospel on their

---

[8] A lay down misere is an unbeatable hand in the card game "500".

terms, often using references to the Qur'an as well as the Bible. Now tracts are great for making the gospel simple, and I would encourage any Christian to have a few up their sleeve to give away, but they are seriously limited. They are great for one-off conversations or street evangelism where there is no relationship involved. They are also useful for answering someone who asks you please to explain the gospel to them. Where tracts fall down is if the person you are talking to has questions that go beyond the tract, or if the person wants to argue the point with you. This is a serious weakness in the case of speaking with Western Muslims because they will almost invariably have questions that go beyond tracts, and will almost invariably want to argue the point with you! You are going to need to have more to say than just a formulaic message you have learnt from memory.

It is important to pause here to make one thing very clear: and that is the difference between evangelism and apologetics. It is crucial for us to remember that people are saved through Christ alone, and that the gospel of Christ is powerful for this (Romans 1:16-17). Our call is to be proclaimers and persuaders, not to be converters. This is evangelism. Apologetics is different. Apologetics is giving good reasons for Christian faith, particularly when you are challenged to provide such reasons. Apologetics uses arguments, rather than simple proclamation. Apologetic arguments can remove obstacles that are preventing faith in Christ, but no-one is saved by an argument. So, for example, if someone believes the Bible to be unreliable, that will be an obstacle to them reading one of the gospels in order to know Jesus. Through an apologetic argument you might convince someone that the Bible is reliable, and once that obstacle is removed they might come to know Jesus through reading a gospel and put their faith in him. Now, our aim must always be to present Christ, not to get into and win arguments. In other words we should seek to do evangelism, rather than seek to get into apologetics. In fact I always say to people in our team: "Use apologetics as a last resort." The problem is that in discussing faith with Muslims you will usually be using your last resort pretty quickly!

So if ongoing evangelistic conversation with a Muslim is likely to be hard work requiring some degree of debate and apologetics, the question for the remainder of this chapter is: how exactly should a Christian speak boldly to a Muslim? What are the sorts of discussions that are likely to facilitate talking about Jesus? What are good questions to ask? What are good topics to cover? What are good points to avoid? What are good terms to use? What are good authorities to appeal to? What are good parts of the Bible to look to for support? What should you say about Muhammad and the Qur'an? What are Muslims going to want to talk about? And, importantly, what arguments are you likely to get into? What apologetic answers will you need to have up your sleeve? There are probably as many of these questions as there are Muslims, and by now you should have gathered that my suggestion is to work it out mainly by getting to know Muslims! But in the following sections I hope to give you a head-start by covering some of the more common issues that, if you can take them on board, should help you to speak boldly even if you are not a natural evangelist, and even if there is every chance that any gospel presentation could lead you into to an apologetic argument.

4.2.   Speak with (your) style

One thing I have noticed over my years in the Christian community is that highly gifted Christian leaders and teachers have a tendency to "theologise" their passions and gifting. By this I mean that we (I say we because I am sure that I theologise, and not because I am sure I am highly gifted!) have a tendency to take our personal faith experiences, or God given callings or passions, or our particular gifting and abilities, and then find a Biblical basis for expecting everyone else to have the same experience, or the same calling, or the same gifting. Sometimes this goes even further. Sometimes we expect others not only to have the same ministry gifting as us, but also the same way, or *style*, of going about doing ministry. I once attended a seminar on sharing the gospel by an obviously gifted evangelist. He suggested that you must *always* begin an evangelistic conversation by confronting people with their sin, and not move on to explaining Jesus' love or forgiveness until they agreed that they were horribly sinful. This sort of approach worked for this guy partly because he had a confrontational personality. And that was fine for him, but is it really true that all people should have that approach? Even if we agree with the theological logic of recognising your sin before seeing a need for saviour, there is no way that we can claim that all evangelism must be done this way. This very gifted guy was theologising from his own gifting and practice, and I suspect that the more passionate, or the more gifted, then the greater the tendency to theologise the stylistic elements of your approach. What makes this an even bigger problem is that those Christians who are suffering from evangelistic inadequacy tend to latch on to copying an "experts" whole approach, including style.

Now the highly gifted experts doing evangelistic ministry to Muslims that I have come across tend to have two distinct approaches or styles to speaking. On the one hand some are incredibly confrontational. One of the most influential of these evangelists in the Muslim world is an Egyptian Coptic priest named Father Zacharia. He is found on internet and satellite TV using extremely polemical arguments against Muhammad and the Qur'an, and his ministry has seen thousands of Muslims enquiring about Jesus and coming to faith. In the same way, for many years now Christians have engaged in debate with Muslims in Hyde Park, London. Both Muslims and Christians yell at the tops of their voices, both Muslims and Christians focus on pointing out the problems with the opposing faith. (Don't read this as a negative – everyone there loves it because they are into this way of talking.) On the other hand, there are those who are incredibly gentle. The man I mentioned in the introduction who wandered the streets was an incredibly gentle and quiet person – despite being a mountain of a man! He was certainly bold in speaking about Jesus at every opportunity, but he did not approach such conversations with confrontation. Another effective evangelist I know has been serving refugees for many years. He has seen many Muslims come to faith in Christ purely through starting with listening to their stories, and then offering to pray for them.

I want to argue that neither of these styles, or any other in between, is right or wrong for speaking with Muslims. Both are used by God, and produce fruit because God uses the particular personality and gifts of individuals. Now you may be thinking 'Hang on, what about what you said in chapter one about persuasion? Didn't you use the sport illustration to point out that using polemics just leads to arguments? Don't you need to go deeper than pointing out negatives if you want to persuade?' Yes! But don't confuse style with content. You can have gentle deep conversations, and you can have high powered and aggressive deep conversations! All the people I have mentioned have done that hard work of getting inside the Muslim heart and mind – often because they are from the same cultural background and naturally understand how to speak to that worldview. When they critique Islam, they critique it in ways that touch hearts because they point out Muslim beliefs that contradict people's deep values.

If you want to speak about Jesus then please don't just copy the approaches you see that you like, or wish you could be like. Do the hard, and sometimes humbling, work of working out your own style and gifting. Do this for your own sake as well as the gospel's because it will save you a lot of pain! If you can't tell what your own style or gifting is then ask someone wise from your church who knows you well – I promise you that they will be able to tell! Once you have worked out your gifting and style, be bold and caring and persevering with it. Maybe you are great at debating and confronting. That's OK, but make sure you are hitting the target with confronting questions that will go somewhere, or debating in a way that tackles key issues for Muslims with arguments that are persuasive. Maybe you like listening and questioning. That's OK too, but make sure you ask good questions that lead to people opening up about the faith issues that really matter to them. Maybe you like telling stories. Again fine, but try and tell the sorts of Jesus stories, or Christian testimonies, that touch hearts.

4.3.   Speak with boldness

Whatever your style, at some point in a discussion with a Muslim you will inevitably disagree about key faith and life issues. These are issues like who Jesus or Muhammad is, or, more confronting, like who goes to heaven and hell and who doesn't. If you are going to have these disagreements it is best to be prepared for it and to have some idea how you are likely to handle it without reneging on being bold (especially if you are not confrontational by nature!). Again this involves some hard work!

First, you will need to have some idea of where you think that Christianity and Islam differ. I mentioned some of the key points of difference in chapter two, but there are plenty of other differences. For example, do you think Christians and Muslims worship the same God? Who do you think Muhammad was? Was he a false prophet deserving condemnation? Was he a remarkable leader who was well meaning but deceived? What do you think about the Qur'an? Is it a completely false document, copied from heretical Jewish and Christian sources, or does it contain some truth about God? I am not saying you need to understand completely a Muslim view on all these things, but you do need to understand that you will end up disagreeing on things like this at some point and you need to be ready to take a stand at that time.

Second, you need to decide how you will go about disagreeing. Will you start with finding as much common ground as possible and disagree at the end, or will you start with pointing out the differences? So, for example, in discussing Jesus you might start by agreeing that he was an amazing prophet, called the Messiah, who did miracles and is coming back to judge – all this is in the Qur'an – but that there is more to the story. Or, on the other hand, you might start by sharing all the things about Jesus that amaze you that are not found in the Qur'an. Similarly, whether you like it or not at some point you will need to have an answer for a Muslim asking your opinion of Muhammad. How you go about such disagreement is your choice, usually based on your style, but to be bold you must be ready to disagree.

Here are a few things I have learnt. Many experts suggest Christians shouldn't express any opinions on Islam, instead pleading ignorance or lack of knowledge of Islam and then just talking about Jesus. This may work in street evangelism, but not in a long term relationship with a Muslim. When you are just getting to know someone, or newly encountering Islam, it can be completely OK to honestly claim not to know the differences, and just talk about your Christian faith. You won't, however, be able to plead ignorance for too long, though, as your Muslim friend may give you some material about Islam. Actually, if you are reading this it is already too late to plead complete ignorance! Similarly many experts advise that we should always avoid saying anything negative about Muhammad because it will offend Muslims. I am not so sure. While it is a bad idea to be rude or abusive about Muhammad (or anyone else for that matter) you must be willing to answer honestly, and boldly, about what you think. If you do not believe Muhammad was a prophet, be prepared to say it. Western Muslims know you don't believe Muhammad was a prophet and will read any polite refusal to say so as weakness in your Christian faith.

4.4. *Speak with shrewdness*

Christians need boldly to take a stand for truth, including at times pointing out error. But I need to warn you to do this intelligently. This is because, as I mentioned in chapter one, *shame and honour* comes into play in Muslim communities, and you must have some awareness of the dynamics of this when telling people they are wrong. I received an insight into this a few years ago when I was with a group of young Muslim men, and one of them told me something I knew for certain was a lie. It was the last in a string of annoyances that week and so I responded by telling him in front of the group that the reason why I would never become a Muslim was because I was sick of the Muslims in our local community lying to me! The response of the wider group surprised me. Instead of defending the young man, or even defending Islam, they turned on the boy and publicly berated him for bringing Islam into disrepute. Was what I did the right thing to do? In retrospect, no. I believe that what I said was true. I even believe that I could have told him that truth in private. The problem here was that by declaring this truth in public I was shaming both the young man and his community. This didn't lead to his, or anyone else's repentance. Instead, it led to an attempt to remove the shame through publicly humiliating the young man. In effect he was forced to carry all the shame personally. It is shrewd

WITNESSING TO WESTERN MUSLIMS

then, when disagreeing with Muslims, to avoid shaming them in front of their family or community, by making them look stupid.

This means you need to be careful in public theological arguments with Muslims. Most Muslims know lots about Islamic practice, but not too much about Islamic theology or history. If you spend even a few hours trawling the internet you will easily be able to come up with a whole lot of theological or historical challenges to Islam that most Muslims will have no understanding of, or answers for. If you try to bring up these challenges it is more likely to shame them for not knowing, or defending, Islam well, than it is to inspire them to seek answers in Christ.

I am not saying there is no place for stumping Muslims with challenging theological questions. In fact Jesus deliberately shamed people like this. He publicly shamed the Pharisees and teachers of the law. He publicly shamed the self-righteous. I believe it is perfectly OK in debates with Muslims who profess to be teachers of, or authorities on Islam, publicly to challenge them as profoundly as possible. I would even be willing to point out hypocritical efforts at self-righteous posturing by ordinary Muslims, but with care. I am not Jesus, and do not have the same insight into hearts as Jesus, so shrewdness is needed in choosing when to speak.

You also need to be smart enough to recognise that when such a *shame and honour* culture is teamed up with a culture of peer pressure you have a recipe for less than open public conversations. Do not expect Muslims to bare their deepest and most honest thoughts in public, and certainly not in front of other Muslims. They will not usually let their community know of any doubts about Islam, or any interest in Christianity. You will need to be shrewd because such guarding of close thoughts and feelings makes people hard to read, and conversations can not be taken at face value. My experience, as a less than subtle Aussie, is that sometimes this can even feel like dishonesty, leading to a lack of trust. Shrewdness, however, might suggest being slow to identify dishonesty, and being quick to appreciate the subtleties of communicating with people who often live in a world of many "faces", and where they share information very selectively because of the community implications.

4.5. Speak with integrity

I mentioned in chapter one that Christians have made a variety of attempts to explain Christianity to Muslims using Muslim terms and concepts. It has become common, even in the West, to hear Christians using Arabic terms when discussing faith with Muslims. Such terms include *Isa* when discussing Jesus, and *injeel* when discussing the Bible/gospels. This is done in an attempt to be "all things" to all Muslims, and while I sympathise with the sentiment, this needs to be approached carefully for at least two reasons. For a start, *Arabic* terms are not always the same as *Muslim* terms. So, for example, "*Isa*" is not the Arabic word for Jesus. The Arabic word for Jesus is "*Yesua*" and is used by Arab Christians. *Isa* is the Muslim name for Jesus found in the Qur'an. This shows that it is important to be careful when contextualizing. Lazy and superficial contextualisation leads to misrepresentations and misunderstandings. You might be thinking this is all a bit picky, but I believe it to be important, because when a Muslim hears you use the word *Isa* rather than Jesus, they are more likely to think that you are starting to think and talk like a Muslim, than to think that it is nice you are trying to speak their language.

A similarly superficial approach to speaking of Christ can be found in some of the tracts gaining "traction" in Muslim ministry around the world. These tracts use verses from the Qur'an to support following Jesus or reading the Bible. There are a few potential problems with using the Qur'an like this. First, there is a very real risk of looking silly by referring to someone else's scripture for support unless you know it extremely well. It is very easy to pluck Qur'an texts – like Bible texts – out of context. However, it is very clear that the overall message of the Qur'an is that Jesus is not to be worshipped, and that the Qur'an supersedes all other scriptures. Muslims know this, and if you try to use the Qur'an out of context to support Christianity you will look ignorant of the true meaning of the Qur'an. In fact if you simply regurgitate a tract without understanding it, it doesn't just look ignorant, it *is* ignorant – but it is common. I recently attended an international mission conference where one of the facilitators "training" people in one such tract admitted that he had never even read the Qur'an! I am not saying that it is always inappropriate to look at the Qur'an with Muslims, but if you simply use a tract approach to pluck out various Qur'an verses without knowing the Qur'an or the context, believe me, you will look silly. I am also not saying that the Holy Spirit doesn't use truths found in the Qur'an to point people to Jesus, as I know of many testimonies where this has happened. However I have also heard the testimony of a Chinese man who, having recently arrived in Australia, went to my old pastor wanting to find out about Jesus. When asked what he knew about Jesus he said that he had learnt about Jesus through watching The Simpsons, and that he had learnt that Jesus was the Son of God who had come to die to take our sins away! Now this is a great proof that God can use anything as a witness, and you might use the Simpsons as an illustrative bridge to the gospel (as I have with youth groups), but you should never claim the Simpsons as a revelatory authority on Jesus.

This leads me to a second, and worse, problem: such an approach lacks integrity. In simplistically appealing to the Qur'an, this approach tries to win arguments (poorly and out of context) by appealing to an authority that Christians don't respect as an authoritative scripture. To help you to see the problem, imagine it the other way round, with Muslims arguing for Islam from the Bible. I once had a conversation in an Islamic centre where one of the staff was trying to convince me that John 14:16 was talking about Muhammad when it promises a coming counsellor (this is a common Muslim belief). When I pointed out to him that not only was that a mistranslation of the verse, but also it completely ignored the context of the Chapter showing the promise referring to the Holy Spirit, his response was: "Well, I don't believe in the Bible anyway. I was only pointing it out because you believe in the Bible and it might persuade you." In the end this sort of superficial attempt at contextualization reveals ignorance, and reeks of a lack of integrity – where ends justify means.

Christian integrity demands that, in our attempts to contextualize, we should be careful not to compromise our message.

57

Always speak about the Christian Christ, not the Muslim Christ. Always appeal to the Bible as your authoritative scripture, not the Qur'an. Never use "the ends justify the means" types of approach. Muslims are aware of such approaches and generally despise these attempts at contextualization as dishonest. Not only that, they will respect you as a Christian far more if you speak of confronting beliefs with passion and truthfulness, rather than trying to make them palatable to Muslim sensibilities. As I have mentioned, Muslims are not precious about faith!

4.6. Speak using questions

Another suggestion is that unless you are speaking with a highly trained Muslim, it is best to talk about personal faith issues, and to avoid abstract theology. A personal example will illustrate why. A while ago I was having a conversation with a young Muslim man and I asked him a theological question. I can't remember the question, but I remember him answering that he didn't know the answer to the question, but that he knew a more mature Muslim man in the local community who might. We visited him, and he too said that he didn't know the answer, but that he could introduce me to a man at the local Islamic centre who might know. I went (alone) to the centre and met this man too, and, again, he said that he didn't know the answer but that the head Imam (teacher) at the centre might, and that he would introduce me to him. Meanwhile the guy I had originally been talking to was back at home!

This taught me an important lesson. Muslim theology and scholarship largely revolves around establishing what is lawful or recommended (or dangerous or forbidden) by God. This is done by knowing the Qur'an and particularly the vast quantity of things said and done by Muhammad which set the boundaries for Muslim behaviour. A Muslim scholar is someone who knows this material well and can apply it to life. If someone is not a scholar they will not try to work things out themselves, but simply ask a scholar. Moreover, if they are asked a question that is not covered by the Qur'an and *sunna* (the teaching and practice of Muhammad) then they will often dismiss it as thus unimportant. This goes back again to what I was saying in chapter one about belief. Islamic knowledge is primarily based on tradition passed on by authorities. Original thought is not highly valued, and questioning outside the bounds given by Islamic tradition and revelation is seen as risky to faith.

The friend I was originally speaking with was a bright guy who was studying at university. At university he questioned and researched. In his faith, he accepted and submitted. This is common among even Western Muslims. My first Arabic lecturer was a PhD student in Chemistry, and was obviously an accomplished scientific thinker and researcher. He was also a passionate Muslim and dedicated promoter of Islam in our classes. Once he was arguing that the Qur'an contained a number of clearly scientific observations of the world that were beyond the human comprehension of the time. I asked him if he could provide me with some evidence of this, so the next class he handed me a printout of a web page with a supposed quote from a Japanese scientist concerning cloud formations. I asked my lecturer where the quote was from and he said he did not know and that it was my job to find out. So much for good research skills! Still, I did a little research of my own and discovered that the quote was a complete fabrication, that the scholar didn't exist, and that his name was made up to the point of being impossible in Japanese. In the end my lecturer had no real interest in researching his faith, instead he simply accepted it. I tell this not to have a go at my lecturer – he was acting in good faith – but to use it as an illustration of the way that most Muslims treat Islamic and scientific knowledge as two totally different forms of knowledge. Islamic knowledge is supreme knowledge, and is self evident, and unquestionable. The practical result of this is that very few Muslims have a deep theological understanding of Islam, and they certainly won't approach theological questions with the independently questioning mind of a Western Christian. How then should we speak about theological questions?

Again, my suggestion is that with Muslims, theology is best discussed in terms of personal faith issues, and it is always best to speak of personal faith issues using questions. It is important to note here that when I say questions I don't mean interrogations! What I do mean is that it is great to ask personal faith questions like: 'What do you think God is like?' 'What is your experience of grace?' 'Does God love you?' 'How does prayer work for you?' 'Do you know God's forgiveness?' 'What difference does your faith make at work/home?' 'Does Ramadan bring lasting change to your life?' 'What do you know about Jesus?' 'What is the Muslim calendar on your wall all about?' 'What is your experience of Christians?' And so on.

These are questions which open up profound issues of faith and theology, and which any Muslim can answer. They are also questions that can easily lead to deep and personal and real conversations, not theological point scoring. Muslims are genuinely concerned about these things. I once attended a Muslim lecture from a world famous Muslim scholar. The crowd was almost all Muslim, and the lecture on Muslim theology went on for close to two hours. After the lecture there was the opportunity for questions, which was taken up with enthusiasm. No-one, however, asked anything about his lecture. The questions I remember were these: "How do I know I am forgiven by God?" "How can I make my husband come home from work and help me parent our kids?" "How can I keep my kids believers and keep them away from drugs and alcohol?" In other words, questions of making faith work in real life. These are things believers of all faiths can talk about. On top of this, asking these types of questions often opens opportunities for Christian testimony.

Here is an example of how. A woman friend of mine was recently in a McDonald's restaurant and noticed a conservatively dressed Muslim woman there with her kids. My friend greeted the woman, who soon was declaring to her both the excellence of Islam, and also how she was being a good Muslim for covering her body so as not to be a temptation for men. My friend then simply replied with a question: 'Don't you think you are drawing more attention to yourself dressed like that?'. This question caused the Muslim woman to pause for thought, and the conversation was able to move on to how sexual temptation worked, to whether men had any responsibility in their sexual desires, and from there to the Bible teaching that men are called to purify their minds and given the Holy Spirit to empower this. This further led to the woman sharing deeply of her personal marriage struggles, and finished with my friend praying with the woman for her and her husband. Please note that my friend's question was not a clever or tricky question designed to win points. But it was a perceptive question that cut to the heart of whether Islam provided the best way of life, moved the woman to reflect on this, and opened the possibility for Christian testimony.

4.7. Speak God's word

Even though it has taken a while to get here, this is my most important point. I believe that our goal should always be to lift Jesus up, not to put Islam down. I once heard Ravi Zacharias say the problem with throwing mud in debates is that everyone gets dirty, and everyone loses ground. I want to be careful here. By now you will know that I am not saying that Christians shouldn't disagree with Muslims, or shouldn't critique Islam, or even shouldn't get into full on and passionate debates with Muslims. What I am saying is that the goal should not simply be to point out error, but to point people to Christ. Knowing what is wrong to believe is important, but still leaves me without truth to cling to. Imagine I am drowning in a sea of broken life rafts. I may need to be told to let go of the raft I am clinging to because it has a hole in it, but that still hasn't saved me. I don't just need to be told which rafts are broken, what I most need is to be told which raft hasn't got a hole in it and will save me. It is the same with faith – in the end I need to know the right way to God. In other words, even if you have had to get into apologetics, always seek to move beyond them to proclamation of God's word. Which parts of God's word? Well, as the Bible says, all scripture is useful for salvation, so you can't get it wrong. However it is a good idea particularly to speak the truths of the gospel that either speak to the felt spiritual needs of Muslims, or that speak of the promises of God that Muslims have little or no experience of from the Qur'an or Islamic teaching. Here are a few examples.

4.7.1. Speak of grace

Although Islam has the concept of grace, it is usually an empty word for Muslims. I once asked a Muslim teacher to explain the word for grace in the Qur'an to me and he said that it was an amazing word.

In fact it was too amazing for him to be able to explain it to me! Similarly, I once spoke at a university to a group of Christians and Muslims. At one point I was speaking about grace when a young Muslim woman got up and challenged me that Islam spoke of God's grace too. I agreed that certainly the word was in the Qur'an, but asked her to tell me how she experienced God's grace personally in her life. She had no answer. The grace found in the Bible, however, is unique because God's grace is not just a word, but is seen in action – most clearly in the life, teaching and cross of Jesus. We need to share with Muslims the multitude of grace images in the Bible. Share Jesus' parables that explain grace (for example, the Pharisee and the Tax Collector, Luke 18:9-14; or the Workers in the Vineyard, Matthew 20:1-16). Share the stories from the four gospels where Jesus acts in grace (for example, visiting Zacchaeus, Luke 19:1-10). Share the promises of God's grace found in the gospel (for example, Romans 3:21-26 or 1 John 4). Share Christian testimonies of receiving and then living out God's grace.

4.7.2. Speak of assurance of forgiveness

Like grace, Muslims have a concept of, and longing for, God's forgiveness. But, like grace, almost no Muslim I have met will ever claim to have assurance of that forgiveness. Speak to them of Jesus' promises that it is through him that forgiveness is certain. Show them Bible verses that speak of assurance, like Ephesians chapter 1 or Romans chapter 8. The searching for, and finding of such assurance is a common refrain in the testimonies of Christians from Muslim backgrounds.

Personal grace and the forgiveness of sin are two Biblical promises concerning our relationship with God that Muslims understand, but that are far richer in the gospel than in Islam. But there are others.

4.7.3. Speak of spiritual cleansing

Muslims have a deep sense of needing cleansing before they can approach God, in fact they must wash before each prayer time. In contrast, the gospel promises a once for all cleansing (for example,

John 15:3, Hebrews 10:19-25), and Jesus is repeatedly seen both coming close to unclean people, and washing them clean (for example, when Jesus healed the ten lepers, Luke 17:11-19, or when Jesus washed the disciples feet, John 13:1-11).

4.7.4. *Speak of the removal of shame*

Similarly, although it is often unfamiliar to Western Christians, the gospel can be powerfully expressed in *shame and honour* terms. Jesus speaks of the last judgement in shame terms (for example, Mark 8:34-38), He is seen shockingly loving shameful people (John 4:1-42), and takes our shame to the cross (Hebrews 12:2). The gospel promises the permanent removal of shame (Romans 9:33, 1 Peter 2:6).

4.7.5. *Speak of the victory of Christ*

Another helpful gospel theme is that of victory. Muslims tend to regard the gospel as weak and the cross as a defeat. It is important not to stop at the crucifixion (which can happen if the focus is always on the forgiveness of sin), but to highlight the triumph of resurrection. Here the gospel promises victory over not just sin and death (1 Corinthians 15:51-57), but also over spiritual powers (Colossians 2:13-15). Again there are many examples from Jesus' ministry of his power over evil spirits (for example, Mark 1:21-28). The gospel promise of victory over spiritual evil is especially important for Muslims who practise a folk Islam where they are highly conscious of demonic and occult practices such as the evil eye. Even in the West there are many Muslims who carry charms, or say prayers, in order to ward off such evil.

4.7.6. *Speak using stories about Jesus, and Jesus stories*

You may have noticed that in each of the above categories I have mentioned both events from Jesus' life as well as verses with clear promises. This is because I think it is important to speak using Jesus' stories – both stories he told, and the events of his life. There are all sorts of good reasons for reading out, or retelling Jesus' parables.

First, Muslims have a respect for Jesus as a prophet, and will often be willing to listen to something he has said. Moreover very few Muslims will be familiar with his teaching so it will be interesting and even intriguing to them. I have had Muslims sitting in tears as I have retold a parable of Jesus that I had become so familiar with that I was almost bored by it! Second, Jesus' stories spoke into a worldview similar to that of Islam, and are well designed to cut to the heart in such a worldview. In fact, living among Muslims has helped me incredibly in understanding Jesus' teaching, especially the Sermon on the Mount. Third, Jesus' stories are usually designed to challenge people to start asking deep faith questions, and there are many stories addressing varieties of faith issues.

4.7.7. *Speak of the depth of sin*

As well as verses about God's nature it is important to be ready to share the verses of the Bible that describe *human nature*. I noted earlier that Muslims have a very optimistic view of human nature, and believe that humans can please God by their obedience. And so if humanity can be obedient, then we do not need a saviour and the incarnation makes no sense. The problem with this is that it doesn't make as much sense of the human experience as the Biblical description of our sinful nature. Again, Jesus' teaching on sin, as in the Sermon on the Mount, is helpful and penetrating. Other good passages for this include Colossians 2:20-23 and Romans 1. (This issue is very foundational in Islam and I have found great resistance among Muslims to acknowledge original sin. Often I will actually encourage Muslims to try to be real Muslims for a week in order to challenge them on this.).

4.7.8. *Speak of your favourite Biblical promises*

Again, this book is not about simple techniques or formulas. It is about how we can testify to the promises in the Bible and particularly the ones that led you to faith in Jesus. Speak about what appeals to you about these promises. Speak about why you believe you can trust them. This brings me to my next point.

4.7.9. *Speak your testimony*

Seek every opportunity to share your testimony. By this I don't just mean how you came to faith, but every aspect of how God is real in your life, and even in the testimonies you hear from other Christians. There are a few reasons why testimonies are powerful in witness.

First, it is worth remembering that, in terms of evidence, all Christians have to rely on in evangelism is testimony to God's actions in history. We don't rely on philosophical proofs for God. We can't point to sinless perfection of Christians. We can't even fully explain the central tenets of our faith like the Trinity, the incarnation and the cross. All we know, and all we can speak of, is that God has turned up in history and in our lives and has done some amazing things. And whatever else we can say, the Bible is our authoritative testimony to these events. This may seem like a weakness, especially when we noted earlier that Muslims like the idea that Islam is clear, simple and sensible, but it seems to me that there is no problem with humans admitting they cannot completely fit God inside their heads. As Christians we don't have all encompassing explanations. We simply testify to the God who created and spoke to Moses on mountains. We testify to the Son who visited in power and grace two thousand years ago. We testify to the Holy Spirit who transforms our lives, and the lives of so many throughout history. This is powerful in that it is glorifying of God, not humanity.

Second, personal testimony is a powerful tool leading to honest and deep relationships and friendship. For a start it is not confrontational. It is highly unlikely that sharing your testimony will lead to an argument or a debate. If you share how you came to faith in Christ your listener is not usually going to say "That is wrong", or "That didn't happen", or "God didn't do that in your life"! Instead your testimony is likely to lead to more questions, or the chance to share deeply about the common human experience of seeking truth about God.

4.7.10. *Speak with preparation*

There are some questions and challenges that you will almost invariably get from nearly all Muslims early on in conversations about faith. In particular, there are three big ones that will come up again and again, and you will need to have some answers up your sleeve. Here are the three:

(1) Muslims will challenge that the Bible has been changed or corrupted.

There are a few different versions of this, with different levels of sophistication. At its most basic level many Muslims think that the fact that there are many different translations of the Bible available means that there are many different Bibles. Alternatively, more sophisticated arguments from some Muslims suggest that there were a whole lot of different Bibles around for the first few hundred years of Christianity until the Council of Nicea standardised the text into what we have now and burned all the alternatives. More complicated again, some Muslims, drawing on recent liberal Biblical scholarship, think that there was an authentic (that is, non-Trinitarian) Jewish Christianity taught by the apostles (for example, The Book of James), but also a corrupted Trinitarian Christianity taught by Paul. The "Pauline" Christians won the day and so we are left with their corrupted Bible. Most Muslims I have spoken to simply repeat one of the above claims without knowing the historical details behind how any of them might have happened. This is partly because they have been taught by their teachers that it is true, and partly because they believe that if the Qur'an is the true and authentic Word of God then when the Bible teaches something different it must have been changed.

(2) Muslims will question how anyone can believe in a Trinity?

This goes back partly to what I said about common sense in Chapter 1. The idea of God being three and one in his very nature is an idea that Christians simply accept on the basis of how God has revealed himself, not because it makes obvious sense, or is easily explainable. It doesn't, and it isn't. Muslims will also point out the fact that the word Trinity is not found in the Bible. The main issue though, for Muslims, stems from the fact that the unity of God is the supreme theological statement of Islam. The Muslim testimony of faith (The *Shahada*) translates literally as *'I testify that there is no God except Allah'*, but what Muslims mean by this is *'I testify that the only God is Allah, who is one'*. This is the pre-eminent belief of Islam. More than this, in the Qur'an this is formulated polemically against polytheists and Christians. The Muslim testimony is not just that "*God is one*". It is that God is one, not many, and not three.

(3) Muslims will ask how God can have a Son?

In part this follows on from the previous point. Muslims who like thinking theologically will argue that if God isn't Trinitarian then it follows that Jesus can't be God's son (at least not in a way different from all humans being God's children). More common however, is the argument that Jesus never referred to himself as God's son.

How should you answer these three challenges?

First, you need to know why you believe these things yourself. You need to ask yourself why you believe the Bible to be unchanged and reliable. What is it about Jesus that makes you believe he is the Son of God? Giving a Muslim an honest answer about what you believe is always better than a winning answer, even if it means admitting that you, too, find it hard to understand how God could be three and one, or how Jesus needed to learn as a child. You may need to do some homework about this!

Second, it is best to answer these challenges in ways that Muslims will understand, and with appeals to the sort of authenticators they recognise. This goes back to what I talked about in Chapter 1 about speaking into different worldviews.

Third, Christians are not provers, we are testifiers. Remember the goal in speaking is not to win arguments, but to testify to truth. With these three things in mind, let me suggest some ideas on how to answer the three particular challenges I have noted.

☐ *Defending of the reliability of the Bible*

Chapter 1 mentioned that Muslims judge historical reliability by whether or not there is an unbroken chain of transmission. This is a

67

problem in defending the historical reliability of the Bible because we don't have that. In fact we can't even say who wrote much of it! Usually Christians appeal to the existence of multiple independent and ancient texts to support historicity, but is that of any use? What should we say? A good place to start is to just say "No, the Bible hasn't been changed." Or "If it was so obvious that the Bible has been changed, do you think I (and millions of others) would base my life on it?" Or again, "Can you show me which bits have been changed?" There is a lot of power in this approach partly because the assertion is true, partly because Muslims accept authoritative testimony (in this case yours!), and partly because giving reasons that people don't understand or agree with just leads to more questions. If you do need to go further I usually say something like: "The books of the original New Testament were written down in many different places, by many different people, and then copied and independently sent around from those places to hundreds of other places all around the ancient world. Even if you wanted to change the New Testament it would have been impossible to collect and change every copy. Not only that, all the copies we have are essentially the same, so there is no evidence whatsoever of deliberate changes." The advantage of this sort of answer is that anyone can understand it because it just tells the story, it doesn't quote scholars or research that no-one has read.

□ *Explaining the idea of a Trinitarian God*

Let's be clear. There is no way to explain fully, or even adequately, the Trinity to anyone, let alone a Muslim who has been taught it is a heresy. I don't believe in the Trinity because I understand it: I believe in a Triune God because I know that whatever God is like, He will be beyond my understanding, and I will need to rely on Him revealing Himself for me to understand anything of Him at all. I believe in God as creator because I see the creation. I believe in God the Son because the things Jesus did and said showed he was the Son. I believe in God the Holy Spirit because of the way I have seen him at work in my life and the lives of others. This is what I say to Muslims because Muslims too believe in a creator God who is supremely transcendent and above our understanding, yet who reveals himself to us. It is important to see the order here. Christianity starts with revelation, not with theology – that's why the word Trinity doesn't appear in the Bible, it is just a word we have come up with to describe the God who reveals Himself. Similarly with Muslims, I will start with Jesus and ask them to examine his life and then decide for themselves whether he was divine.

☐ *Establishing Jesus as the Son of God*

This question is really just the trinity question from an earthly angle. Earthly because it suggests to Muslims the offensive idea that God would taint himself by getting involved with human sexuality (sometimes they think Mary is regarded by Christians as a person of the Trinity). The best way to tackle this question is to ask them a question: "What do you mean by Son of God?" This is a good question because usually Muslims misunderstand the term, and usually you will be able to agree with them that God would not have sex with Mary, or that God could not physically have a son. Often this will lead to a chance to explain what we really mean by the term Son of God. But what exactly do we mean? For Christians the term Son of God is not a physical or genetic term, like offspring, but is a relational and an honorific title, like Prince. It is an important term because it links Jesus to the prophecies that the Messiah would be a descendent of David, and Jesus is spoken of by God in the same way (Psalm 2). In other words 'Son of God' is a similar title to Messiah. This way of understanding the idea is helpful for Muslims because they already believe that Jesus is the Messiah, and that Messiah is an honorific title (even though I have commonly found that they don't understand what a Messiah is!).

Make sure you know the key Biblical passages concerning Jesus' divinity, and the reliability of the Bible. Muslims may want to take issue, but at the very least you need to be able to point to the reasons for your faith in these things. John's writing is useful concerning Jesus' divinity (especially John 8 & 14 and 1 John 1), and I have found 1 Corinthians 15:1-11 very handy concerning the historicity of the gospel. Please note that these answers are not likely to satisfy many Muslims immediately. I believe, though, that they start the conversation off on the right foot, and lead in helpful directions.

KEY POINTS:

o   *The goal in conversation must always be to give good reasons for faith in Christ, not to get into, or win, arguments. You will often need to engage in bold apologetics.*

o   *Always look for opportunities to share Biblical stories or promises concerning the day to day faith issues that are important to Muslims.*

o   *There are some topics you will need to be prepared to talk about: particularly the Trinity, Jesus as the Son of God, and the reliability of the Bible.*

---

5.   Remembering...

*"I want to remind you of the gospel I preached to you,
which you received and on which you have taken your stand."*

1 Corinthians 15:1

In this little book I have repeatedly pointed to the thought and
preparation involved in witnessing to people with different religious
worldviews. There has been lots of stuff about working hard, thinking
hard, living appropriately, and speaking carefully. Having said all that
there are three things I want to finish with, to remind us that
Christian witness is not all about us and our efforts.

5.1.   Conversion is God's work

Conversion is God's work, not ours. It is the Holy Spirit that opens
hearts and draws people to Christ, not our persuasion (John 16:8). It
is the gospel that is the power for salvation, not our techniques,
approaches, or arguments (Romans 1:16-17). Our efforts can be tools
in the Holy Spirit's hands, but we are neither indispensable, nor able
to ruin God's plans. So relax! And pray. Prayer for your Muslim
friends, neighbours and colleagues is the most effective evangelistic
tool you have, so use it.

5.2.   Spiritual warfare is real

Building the Kingdom of Heaven is a supernatural spiritual battle,
and battles are tough. Spiritual strongholds are tough to break down.
The community and religious pressures I have talked about are heavy
and potentially dangerous to exiting Muslims. The eternal stakes are

high. Do not underestimate the spiritual nature of witnessing. The battle you enter is much bigger than you are. Do not be surprised when witnessing is discouraging, slow or even personally wounding. Do not rely on your own strength. Make sure you use God's weapons (Ephesians 6:10-20). Always make sure you ask your church to pray!

5.3. Muslims do come to faith!

Finally, after all this you may have the impression that witnessing to Muslims seems so hard that it is not worth the effort. Maybe you feel that it is too complicated, that the Muslim mindset is too different, or there is too little fruit. But this would be a mistake. There is no one beyond the reach of God's grace. There is no-one too hard for, or far away from, God – including Muslims. The worldwide church has only recently started seriously to invest prayer and thought and resources into understanding and reaching the Muslim world. But even now there are literally hundreds of thousands of people from Muslim backgrounds coming to faith all around the world – including from some Muslim people groups that are reputed to be highly resistant to the gospel. I have met many of them, and some are very close friends. Their Christian testimonies are varied, and some are amazing, but they all carry a common thread. They all met Jesus through encountering his Word, and the witness of ordinary believers who loved them and testified faithfully to them. If this little book has encouraged you on the road to being one of those 'ordinary believers', it will have answered my prayers for it.

"May the grace of the Lord Jesus Christ, and the love of God, and the fellowship of the Holy Spirit be with you."

2 Corinthians 13:14

LATIMER PUBLICATIONS

LATIMER PUBLICATIONS

Lightning Source UK Ltd.
Milton Keynes UK
UKOW05f0503221113

221551UK00002B/73/P